Apples: Old and New Varieties
Heirloom Apple Varieties

by US Dept. of Agriculture

with an introduction by Roger Chambers

This work contains material that was originally published in 1913.

This publication was created and published for the public benefit, utilizing public funding and is within the Public Domain.

This edition is reprinted for educational purposes and in accordance with all applicable Federal Laws.

Introduction Copyright 2017 by Roger Chambers

Self Reliance Books

Get more historic titles on animal and stock breeding, gardening and old fashioned skills by visiting us at:

http://selfreliancebooks.blogspot.com/

Introduction

I am pleased to present yet another title on Gardening.

The work is in the Public Domain and is re-printed here in accordance with Federal Laws.

As with all reprinted books of this age that are intended to perfectly reproduce the original edition, considerable pains and effort had to be undertaken to correct fading and sometimes outright damage to existing proofs of this title. At times, this task is quite monumental, requiring an almost total "rebuilding" of some pages from digital proofs of multiple copies. Despite this, imperfections still sometimes exist in the final proof and may detract from the visual appearance of the text.

I hope you enjoy reading this book as much as I enjoyed making it available to readers again.

Roger Chambers

BULLETIN No. 361.

APPLES: OLD AND NEW.

U. P. HEDRICK AND G. H. HOWE.

INTRODUCTORY.

The culture of new varieties is looked upon by conservative fruit-growers as gambling, pure and simple. Several causes combined put this stigma on new fruits: Introducers outrun all license in describing their wares; nurserymen too often rename old varieties; and, more than all else, originators, nurserymen, and fruit-growers have wrong ideals and introduce varieties without value or to fill places better occupied by existing sorts which cannot be dislodged.

Yet despite the hazards, novelties must be grown if fruits are to be improved. There are many notions current that old varieties can be changed for the better but the statements to this effect far outstrip the evidence. Varietal improvement has been and will probably remain a negligible factor in obtaining better fruits and new varieties must be grown to keep up the evolution which each generation has seen in fruits and which will continue indefinitely since the limits of improvement can never be reached.

Old varieties are novelties in new locations as they are also to all who have never grown them. The introduction of new sorts and the uncertainty as to old ones makes it necessary for some one to grow varieties on probation in fruit-growing regions. Now to test varieties of fruits is a money-taking, time-consuming task which requires not only the good judgment of an expert fruit-grower but wide and thorough knowledge of varieties. Manifestly, it is work for an experiment station and not for an individual.

The New York Station attempts to test every variety of fruit obtainable that will thrive in this climate. This bulletin is one of several publications from this Station giving results of tests of old and new apples. It is the latest answer to the oft-repeated question: "What apples shall I plant?"

The most valuable information for the grower is to be found in the catalog of apples on the last pages of the Bulletin. Studying the varieties under test has thrown light on several phases of apple-growing, some of them more suited to controversy than practice yet worth taking into account, and these are discussed before the catalog is reached under the heads: Groups of Apples, Strains of Apples, Do Apples Degenerate, Natural Resistance to Disease in Apples, and Seedless Apples.

GROUPS OF APPLES.

Horticultural writers very commonly divide apples into vaguely-defined divisions called "groups." This term, like "kinds," "strains," "races," and "sorts," has no official recognition in the botanical or horticultural codes of nomenclature, and since the codes of botany and horticulture are already complex even to experts, it would be confounding confusion to add this term officially. But we can hardly expect to have uniformity in the nomenclature of plants, wild or cultivated; and since "group" is a word of great convenience to fruit-growers and is understood alike by those who use it and those to whom it is addressed, convenience, in this case, can well be put before principle and the use of "groups" be continued.

The limits of the term are easily set; indeed, its application is so apparent in pomology that it hardly needs defining. A *group* is a collection of varieties of a fruit which has so many characters in common that near kinship is apparent. Members of groups of apples usually have a common ancestor, one, two, or at most, three generations back. So used, a group is a fraction of the species, the true botanical unit, and a variety is a fraction of the group.

The formulation of varieties of apples into groups in accordance with their blood relationships is, in one particular, at least, of prime importance to apple-growers; since groups of apples have marked adaptations to particular conditions. Thus, the Winesap, Romanite and Ben Davis groups are preeminently adapted to southern apple regions; the Fameuse, Blue Pearmain, Reinette and Baldwin groups to New York; and the crab-hybrid group, represented by Wealthy, and the Russian apples, for the north Mississippi Valley. This development of groups of related varieties for regions having diverse conditions is becoming more and more marked and in New York we can discard whole divisions from the State and in the State can assign certain groups to certain pomological districts. Grouping varieties, then, is not only a means of classification but is a real help many times as a guide to apple-growers in seeking what to plant.

Groups are by no means fixed units. If the species of fruits were fixed they might be divided into parts that would be definite. But species are "judgments," to use an oft-quoted saying of Asa Gray, and the division of the apple species must also be an act of judgment, the value of which depends upon the knowledge of the judge. The groups of apples which follow, then, are tentative, subject to modification, and are presented chiefly as a means of showing the adaptations of varieties.

GROUPS OF APPLES.

Aport group. — Large, handsome, fall apples, coarse in texture and of medium quality. Some members of the group are adapted to all parts of New York.

Alexander,	Bismarck,	McMahon,
Ananarnoe,	Constantine,	Thompson,
Aport Orient,	Great Mogul,	Wolf River.
Arabka,	Howard Best,	
Bietigheimer,	Judson,	

Baldwin group. — Highly colored, long keeping, well flavored, rather large apples with similarities in texture, flavor, form and color markings. Trees winterkill in the northern districts but are well adapted to all other districts.

Arctic,	Barber,	Red Russet (red strain
Babbitt,	Hunterdon,	of Baldwin),
Baldwin,	Olympia (identical	Sutton,
Bayard,	with Baldwin),	Tufts.

Ben Davis group.— Rather large, bright red, coarse and solid in texture, indifferent flavor, thick skin, shipping well and keeping well.

Arkansas Beauty,	Coffelt,	Saratoga,
Beach,	Collins,	Schenectady,
Ben Davis,	Dickinson,	Shackelford,
Black Ben Davis,	Eicke,	Shirley,
Challenger,	Florence,	Wallace Howard.
Chicago,	Gano,	

Black Gilliflower group.— Medium sized, dark red, oblong, ribbed apples of good quality but rather dry and coarse in texture. Less hardy than the Baldwin group. Particular as to soils.

Black Gilliflower,	Lady Finger,	Striped Gilliflower.
Deacon Jones,	Scollop Gilliflower,	
Johnsonite,	Skelton,	

Blue Pearmain group.— Somewhat large, dull red with bluish bloom, mild flavor, fair quality, dense texture and thick skins. Adapted to northern conditions and for most part valuable there only.

Baxter,	Mabie,	Scarlet Beauty,
Bethel,	Monroe Sweet,	Stone,
Blue Pearmain,	Oel Austin,	Victoria Sweet,
Du Bois,	Perry,	Windsor.
Gideon Sweet,	Perry Red,	
Jewett Red,	Rutledge,	

Chenango group.— Medium sized, red striped, oblong conic apples of high quality, peculiar aroma and delicate texture. In general the three sorts in this group succeed where the Baldwin can be grown.

Chenango,	Prince Double,	Stump.

Early Harvest group.— Summer apples of medium size, pale yellow or white in color, of good but not superior quality and with delicate breaking flesh. More suitable to the warmer than to the colder portion of the State.

Early Harvest,	Early Ripe,	Parry White.

Fameuse group.—Medium sized, handsome red, usually striped, apples, roundish oblate, thin skinned, of high dessert quality, and pure white tender flesh. A tendency to reproduce true from seed is a striking peculiarity. As a group, predisposed to fungus troubles. The varieties in this group, with one or two exceptions, reach their highest perfection in the North. The most valuable group for the colder portion of the State.

Boys Delight,	Jersey Black,	St. Lawrence,
Canada Baldwin,	La Victoire,	Shiawassee,
Cortland,	Louise,	Striped Fameuse,
Detroit Red,	McIntosh,	Switzer,
Fameuse,	Onondaga,	Scarlet Pippin,
Hilaire,	Otsego,	Ver.

Hibernal group. — Probably the hardiest apples. Mature in a short season. Russian.

Bogdanoff Glass,	Hibernal,	Ostrakoff,	Romna.

Jonathan group. — Medium sized, handsome red apples of high quality, and crisp, juicy flesh. Variable in adaptations. Resembles the Baldwin group. With one or two exceptions best adapted to the Eastern districts.

Esopus,	King David,	Red Canada,
Flushing *Spitzenburg*,	McCroskey,	Rensselaer,
Jonathan,	Manchester,	Rockland.
Kaighn,	Mother,	

Keswick group. — English apples of unknown adaptations in New York.

Keswick, Lord Suffield.

Lady group. — Very small, roundish oblate, dessert apples, handsome in color and sprightly in quality, with crisp, juicy flesh, thin skin, and good keeping qualities. Best adapted to the Hudson Valley and Long Island districts.

Highland,	Peron,	Star Lady.
Lady,	Sleight,	

Lawver group. — Medium sized, of very high color, rather dense, medium coarse texture and inferior flavor. Excellent keepers. From the South, but Akin, at least, is worth trying in the milder parts of New York.

Akin,	Lawver,	McAfee.

Limbertwig group.— From the Southwest and not adapted to New York conditions.

    Green Limbertwig,   Red Limbertwig.

Longfield group.— Russian, and can be grown in practically all parts of New York.

    English Pippin,   Longfield.

Lowland Raspberry group.— Russian. Adapted to Northern New York.

    Lowland Raspberry,   Red Wine.

Newtown Spitzenburg group.— Medium sized, roundish, striped apples of high quality. Running small in New York and not well adapted to any of our districts.

Bethlehemite,	Duncan,	Newtown Spitzenburg.

Northern Spy group.— Large, striped red, roundish oblate, ribbed, with delicate bloom, juicy, crisp, fine grain, of highest flavor and quality. Fastidious as to soils but probably can be grown in congenial locations in all but the coldest portions of the State.

Arnold,	Northern Spy,	Stanard,
Doctor,	Ontario,	Wagener.
Hagloe,	Oswego,	
Melon,	Schoharie,	

Oldenburg group.— Medium to above in size, variously striped with red, generally ripening in fall and of comparatively short season. Tart, culinary apples with but few dessert sorts. Russian. Probably the most cosmopolitan of the groups here listed — some members succeeding in all parts of New York.

Anis Rose,	Falix,	Okabena,
Autumn Streaked,	Gladstone,	Oldenburg,
Borovinka,	Golden White,	Pewaukee,
Buda,	Hoadley,	Striped Winter,
Champaign,	Lead,	Zolotareff.
Charlamoff,	Lou,	
Dudley,	Milwaukee,	

GRAVENSTEIN SECTION.

    Banks,   Gravenstein.

Ralls group. — On mature trees medium to below in size, rather dull striped red, of superior quality and texture, keeping late, productive to a fault. A southern group not adapted to northern conditions.

Doctor Walker,	Milam,	Salome.
Ingram,	Ralls,	

Rambo group. — Only medium in size, roundish oblate, rather dull striped red, good quality. Southern. Adaptations not well known for New York, though some members of the group can be grown in the warmer districts of the State.

Domine,	Milden,	Wells.
Lacker,	Rambo,	

Red Astrachan group. — Summer apples of above medium size, crisp, tart and of good quality. May be grown in all parts of the State.

Oszi Vaj,	Red Astrachan,	White Astrachan.

Reinette group. — With few exceptions rather large in size, of green or yellow ground color, with or without blush, and generally of good quality. A large and poorly defined group which is here divided into four sections. Nearly all of the members, with the exception of a few in the Newtown Section, thrive in New York. Only a few varieties of this group, however, succeed in the northern district.

FALL PIPPIN SECTION.

Albion,	Greenville,	Peach Blow,
Boiken,	Hawley,	Reinette Pippin,
Crowns,	Holland Pippin,	Sharp,
Elgin Pippin,	Jack,	White Spanish,
Ewalt,	Lowell,	Winter Banana,
Fall Harvey,	Maiden Blush,	Winter Pippin,
Fall Pippin,	Magenta,	York Pippin.
French Pippin,	Newark Pippin,	
Golden Pippin,	Ohio Pippin,	

RHODE ISLAND GREENING SECTION.

Autumn Swaar,	Holland Winter,	Sheddan,
Battyani,	Monmouth,	Starr,
Bottle Greening,	Northwestern Greening,	Sweet Greening,
Canada Reinette,	Patten,	Tobias Pippin,
Fall Orange,	R. I. Greening,	Victuals and Drink.

NEWTOWN SECTION.

Admirable,	Ivanhoe,	Slingerland,
Belmont,	Middle,	Westchester,
Clinton,	Peck *Pleasant*,	White Pippin,
Green Newtown,	Perry Russet,	Yellow Newtown.
Grimes,	Pickard,	
Huntsman,	(I) Shannon,	

SWAAR SECTION.

Mann,	Seneca Favorite,	Swaar.

Romanite Group.— Variable in size, highly colored, from poor to good in quality, keeping very late. Southern apples of little value in New York with the possible exception of one or two sorts for the warmer districts.

Buckingham,	Minkler,	Pennock,
Gilpin,	Missing Link,	Romanite,
Glenloch,	Mock,	Stark,
Lansingburg,	Nero,	York Imperial.

Rome group.—Above medium in size, roundish, handsomely colored apples of indifferent quality. Rome, only, succeeds in some parts of New York.

Ben Hur,	Langford,	Rome.

Russet group.— Ranging from small to above medium in size, russet colored, with peculiarly fine-grained, dense texture, sprightly flavor and good keeping quality. Illy defined as to adaptations but some member succeeding in all of the New York districts.

Brownlees,	Golden Russet,	Roxbury,
Bullock,	Hunt Russet,	Sailee Russet,
Carpentin,	Long Island Russet,	Swayzie,
English Russet,	Pomme Grise,	Sweet Russet.

Summer Rambo group.— Large, attractively striped with red, roundish oblate, coarse in texture, and of average quality, ripening in early fall. Adaptations not well defined for New York.

Grosh,	Summer Rambo,	Western Beauty.

Sweet Bough group.— Summer or fall apples of sweet flavor, medium to large size, variably conic, good quality. Very general in adaptations, although some of the members cannot be grown in cold localities.

Autumn Bough,   **Fullerton Sweet,**   **Sweet Bough.**

Tetofsky group.— Summer apples, below medium in size, striped, of average quality. Valuable only in cold climates.

July,   **Tetofsky.**

Tompkins King group.— Early winter apples, large, attractively striped with red, variable but symmetrical in form, of superior quality and characteristic dense, coarse texture and aromatic, yellowish flesh. Especially suited to the western New York districts, but succeeding to a fair degree in all except the most northern districts.

Adirondack,	**Halt,**	**Palouse,**
Blenheim,	**Hubbardston,**	**Ribston,**
Ensee,	**Ozone,**	**Tompkins King.**
Fishkill,		

Twenty Ounce group.— Large, late fall, broadly splashed red apples, roundish in form, of good quality and with a coarse, yellowish, aromatic flesh. Grown more or less generally in all but the most northern districts.

Collamer,   **Lyscom,**   **Twenty Ounce.**

Vandevere group.— Local in adaptation and confined mostly to the warmer part of the State.

Ronk,   **Vandevere,**   **Vandevere Improved (identical with Vandevere).**

Wealthy group.— Fruit undersized on old trees. Early and abundant croppers. Hardy and adapted to all of the apple districts of New York.

Peter, Wealthy, and several Minnesota seedlings.

Winesap group.— Winter apples, medium to large in size, dark red, rather solid and of fine grain, of good but not high quality, good keepers. A group belonging to the South and West and of small importance in any of the apple districts of New York.

Arkansas,	Oliver,	Winesap,
Arkansas Black,	Paragon,	Winter Paradise.
Kinnaird,	Stayman Winesap.	

Yellow Bellflower group.— Medium to large apples, characteristically oblong conic, predominantly yellow, with a large somewhat remarkably open core. Flesh firm, crisp, aromatic and of high quality for culinary purposes. Somewhat general in distribution throughout the State but inclining to the southern and warmer districts.

Barry,	Moyer,	Summer Bellflower,
Flory,	Newman,	Titus Pippin,
Kirtland,	Occident,	Yellow Bellflower.
Mason Orange,	Ortley,	

Yellow Transparent group.— Early summer apples, of medium size and characteristically thin skin and tender flesh. Russian. Adapted to all New York districts.

Breskovka, Red Transparent, Thaler, Yellow Transparent.

STRAINS OF APPLES.

As dividing the species into groups of varieties helps in determining adaptations and, therefore, what to plant; so, the division of the variety into strains may be helpful if the strains are real and not fanciful — as proves so often to be the case. Strains arise through bud variations, long known to fruit-growers as sports, but recently dignified by De Vries as mutations. Strains so arising, in apples, in particular, usually differ from the parent variety in one or at most but a few characters. Color of fruit seems to be the character which is in a mutating condition in apples; and nearly all of the strains of this fruit differ from the parent only in color. The touchstone which Nature uses in creating new characters in plants has not yet been discovered and there are no known means whereby a variety may be made by man to sport or mutate.

Three varieties out of the 804 catalogued in this Bulletin have probably originated as bud-mutations. Each of these three differs from its parent only in the color of the fruit and ought to be rated as a strain rather than as a distinct variety. Each not only so strongly resembles the parent as scarcely to be distinguished from it, but answers the same purpose, is adapted to the same environment and will probably sell in the markets under the parental name, though in two of the three cases the apples ought to sell better by reason of the higher color.

The three apples are Banks, a bright red mutation of Gravenstein, Collamer, a highly colored offshoot of Twenty Ounce, and Red Russet, the well known russet variation of Baldwin. The first two strains are improvements on the parents but the russet Baldwin has no merits superior to its parent. In the last case, at least, the strain is not well fixed, since buds from Russet Baldwins occasionally produce normal Baldwins and individual trees are reported in which part of the product is russet and the remainder the normal red.

It is possible that Green and Yellow Newtown and Black Ben Davis and Gano are related as parent and mutant offspring. At the most, however, there is only the slightest possible distinction — a case of tweedledum and tweedledee — in either of the two pairs. In neither pair is there a claim as to which was parent or which offshoot. The high color in Yellow Newtown and Black Ben Davis, if it exist, would in most markets be a commercial asset.

As the writer has tried to show elsewhere,[1] deviations from type which can be perpetuated are exceedingly rare. Fluctuating variations due to environment there are in countless numbers, but these are not known to be transmitted and probably disappear with a change in environment.

The introduction of some fluctuating variation or a new variety is not uncommon in apples, this catalog furnishing several examples. Thus, Improved Wagener, heralded as a " pedigreed " strain of the common Wagener differs not a whit from its parent

---

[1] N. Y. Agr. Expt. Sta. Bul. 350: pp. 146 to 151. 1912.

on our grounds; Olympia, another "pedigreed" marvel of the press "bred up" from the Baldwin is a "chip off the old block," a typical Baldwin, as it grows here; Improved Shannon and Improved Vandevere are other examples of "pedigreed strains" in which no improvement can be found when the trees are grown side by side with the parents. These are but a few examples cited to lead up to a caution several times sent out from this Station in the past few years: Fruit-growers should steer clear of "pedigreed stock" and "improved strains" of varieties until the new productions can be seen somewhere by competent judges growing side by side with the parents. So far, improved strains have turned out to be better suited to advertising than to the needs of fruit-growers.

DO APPLES DEGENERATE?

We are not breaking new ground in considering this question, as it is at least a century old. Knight, foremost of horticulturists a hundred years go, maintained that varieties of cultivated plants deteriorate with age. He held that, since all the individuals of any variety of a plant propagated by vegetative means are only parts of one original plant, however greatly multiplied or widely scattered, all must simultaneously approach old age and death. There has been scarcely a horticulturist of note since who has not pronounced for or against Knight's view, in some one of its many phases. If plant-growers were allowed to settle the controversy the verdict would be unanimous that "varieties do degenerate." But the trend of science is against degeneration of varieties.

Science says that varieties retain their characters permanently, suffering deterioration neither from old age nor oft-repeated vegetative reproduction. Cells and plants may die in millions from various causes but individuals retain the power to reproduce the variety indefinitely. Perhaps a qualification to this statement should be made. It is possible that new varieties, especially those arising from crosses, have a first flush of vigor and are more or less unstable, or do not show all of their characters in the first few years of their existence.

It is desirable that experience with a particular plant extending over a long period should be put on record if it have a bearing on this matter of degeneracy. Most of the apples discussed in this Bulletin have been grown on the Station grounds. The origin, history, description and statements of faults and merits from textbooks, the press and correspondents, are on file and in daily use. When all the information from these sources, made plain by familiarity, is focused, stability rather than variation characterizes varieties of apples.

The following varieties, in particular, have been studied in the orchard and in the literature. The Baldwin has been under cultivation since about 1740, yet trees on our grounds, from several sources, show no signs of deterioration. Though Baldwin is the most widely planted apple in America, the whole progeny of the original tree, with the exception of the Russet Baldwin, a mutation, is uniformly the same when grown under identical conditions. A Rhode Island Greening tree in the Station orchard propagated from what is supposed to be the original Rhode Island Greening, about 200 years old, is the same in growth and bears apples no better, no worse, than trees several generations removed from the parent plant. The Roxbury Russet, Lady and Fameuse, all grown for three centuries, show no impairment of vigor or change in characters if we may compare growing plants with the descriptions in old textbooks.

Varieties known to be over 200 years old, beside the three named, trees of which still grow vigorously and produce well, are Ribston, Green Newtown, Holland Winter, Pomme Grise, Winter Pearmain and Yellow Bellflower. Of those over 100 years there are a score or more of well known sorts whose history and behavior are so well recorded as to leave little doubt that they are the same now as in the beginning. If they are wearing out it is a very slow process. Among these are Fall Pippin, Gloria Mundi, Hawley, Williams, Early Harvest, Detroit Red, Oldenburg, Red Astrachan, Maiden Blush, Porter, St. Lawrence, Sweet Bough, Black Gilliflower, Ben Davis, Cooper Market, Domine, Esopus

Spitzenburg, Grimes, Hubbardston, Jonathan, Peck Pleasant, Ralls, Red Canada, Smith Cider, Swaar, Tompkins King, Wagener, Westfield, and Winesap.

The fact that many of the varieties named are less popular than they once were and that other apples famous in their day have disappeared, argues nothing. Varieties thus drop out because they are outclassed by newcomers. Of the sorts named, some will be cited as lacking in vigor, as "losing in constitution." These, it will be found, have been "defectives" or "unmanageables" from the start. It was the great excellency of their product that originally brought them from the limbo of unnamed seedlings. Varieties disappear in localities, too, because they are out of harmony with their surroundings.

The fruit-grower sees individual trees wearing out and jumps to the conclusion that the variety is running down. Individual trees wear out by the million because of neglect, unsuitable soil, insects and diseases. The effects of the causes named can no more be attributed to degeneracy than the ills and ailments of mankind due to poor diet, care and surroundings can be said to come from degeneracy in mankind.

It is true, as every nurseryman well knows, that debility in the parent stock is transmitted in some degree to the succeeding generation — a matter of feed and not of breed — but this effect does not continue through more than a few years if the cause be removed. The weakling from a poorly nourished bud usually outgrows its frailness and none of it is passed on to future generations.

From all evidence to be had it would seem that the fruit-grower is safe in assuming that for practical purposes varieties of apples do not degenerate. Neither do they change. Vigor cannot be permanently increased, nor characters resulting from environment added, by using the sieve of selection. But through the horn of plenty, vigor can be increased for the generation in hand and trees may be made to take on for the time being new and oftentimes valuable characters. Abundance of food, the best of care, protection against insects, diseases, adverse soil or adverse climate are the means of preventing individual degeneracy which so many fruit-growers confound with degeneration of the variety.

NATURAL RESISTANCE TO DISEASE IN APPLES.

Notes on resistance to the various troubles of apples have been taken in the Station orchard for a number of years and while these, when compiled, make no great showing, yet they do have some value to apple-growers. It means much in selecting varieties to know which are immune or susceptible to an uncontrollable disease, as fire blight; or in the planting of home orchards, where it may not be feasible to spray, a man may well select the sorts that are least susceptible to scab, whereas this disease counts for almost nothing to those who spray. The subject, as one can see after a moment's thought, is a most important one to plant-breeders.

Immunity to contagious disease, or the fact that some animals and plants are more or less secure against infectious germs to which their near of kin are subject, is elementary knowledge alike to those who have charge of the health of humans or of lower forms of life. In spite of a wealth of recent discoveries the causes and conditions of immunity are not well known. With plants, especially, knowledge of causality and condition is a thing of shreds and patches. It is known, however, that there are two kinds of immunity; that which is acquired and that which is inherited.

Immunity in animals is acquired in several ways; as, by having the disease, of which smallpox and measles are examples; by being inoculated with attenuated virus or with some toxic product of the bacteria; and by injections of the serum of some other immune animal. Immunity in plants takes a different turn and it is not known that it can be acquired. Man has smallpox but once, but there is no known parallel in the plant kingdom; though there are cases, as that of pear blight, in which a disease seldom attacks old plants which must have had the disease in their youth. Neither is it possible to cause immunity in plants by vaccinations, inoculations or injections.

Inherited immunity is possessed by animals and plants alike. Negroes are immune to yellow fever; some cattle and sheep to anthrax; certain pears and apples are immune to blight; some peaches to leaf-curl. Immunity sometimes belongs to species, sometimes to races or varieties and sometimes to individuals.

But while we are in comparative ignorance of how immunity is transmitted we now have a substantial body of facts showing that it can be bred in plants. As far back as 1900, in the medieval days, almost the prehistoric days, of plant breeding, as we view the progress that has since been made, the breeding of disease-resistant plants had been begun and has been steadily carried on since through selection and by crossing. Through selection Blinn[1] has developed a cantaloupe resistant to blight; Bolley[2] has bred a flax resistant to flax wilt; Bain and Essary[3] a red clover that withstands a fungus; Jones[4] has selected a potato resistant to late blight; and Orton[5] has grown a cowpea resistant to a wilt fungus. The work done with these plants should be most suggestive to breeders of apples.

Not so much has been done through hybridizing but still a very promising start has been made. Orton[6] has grown a hybrid between the watermelon and the citron which is resistant to the watermelon wilt, while Biffen[7] has made the most important dis-

---

[1] Blinn, P. K. A rust-resisting cantaloupe. Colo. Agr. Exp. Sta. Bull. 104. N 1905.

[2] Bolley, H. L. Breeding for resistance or immunity to disease. *Proc. Amer. Breeders' Assoc.* 1: 131-135. 1905.

[3] Bain, S. M., and Essary, S. H. Selection for disease-resistant clover. Tenn. Agr. Exp. Sta. Bull. 75. D 1906.

[4] Jones, L. R. Disease resistance of potatoes. U. S. Dept. Agr. Pl. Ind. Bull. 87. 1905.

[5] Orton, W. A. The wilt disease of the cowpea and its control. U. S. Dept. Agr. Pl. Ind. Bull. 17: 9-22. 1902.

[6] Orton, W. A. A study of disease resistance in watermelons. Science II. 25: 228. 1907.

[7] Biffen, R. H. Mendel's laws of inheritance and wheat breeding. *Jour. Agr. Sci.* 1: 4-48. 1905.

———. Studies in the inheritance of disease resistance. *Jour. Agr. Sci.* 2: 109-128. Ap. 1907.

covery that resistance and susceptibility in one species are Mendelian characters. He has found that susceptibility in wheat to attacks of yellow rust are inherited in Mendelian ratio. If his conclusions are correct, susceptibility to this rust is a unit-character in wheat; immunity depends upon the absence of this character.

Biffen's evidence is such that we are forced to accept it for this disease of wheat. When we supplement his discovery with the knowledge we previously had of inheritance of disease, we are filled with hope that immunity and susceptibility are inheritable characters with many diseases of plants.

It will not do to jump immediately to the conclusion that we shall shortly breed fruits resistant to all fungi and bacteria. The task will be long and laborious for any one disease, as it can be accomplished only by breeding new varieties — old sorts cannot be changed. Varieties having immunities must be crossed with other varieties. With the manifold characters of the two parents, it may require much shuffling and many draws to secure the combination of disease resistance with other characters that a good variety must have.

Meanwhile, not much real building can be done until we have the foundation laid. That foundation must be knowledge of the immunities and susceptibilities of existing varieties. The chief object of this brief discussion of resistance to disease is to introduce a list of varieties of apples which at the Geneva Experiment Station are more or less resistant or susceptible to two diseases — apple scab (*Venturia inaequalis* [Cooke] Aderh.) and apple blight (*Bacillus amylovorus* [Burr.] De Toni).

Susceptibility of Apples to Apple Scab.

Relatively immune.	*Relatively susceptible.*
Alexander,	Belmont,
Baxter,	Bellflower,
Ben Davis,	Chenango,
Black Gilliflower,	Esopus Spitzenburg,
Cranberry Pippin,	Fall Pippin,
Gano,	Fameuse,

Relatively immune.	*Relatively susceptible.*
Gravenstein,	Golden Pippin,
Grimes,	Green Newtown,
Hubbardston,	Hawley,
Jonathan,	Huntsman,
Northwestern Greening,	Lady,
Oldenburg,	Lady Sweet,
Red Astrachan,	Lawver,
Rome,	Maiden Blush,
Roxbury Russet,	McIntosh,
Sutton,	Mother,
Swaar,	Northern Spy,
Tolman Sweet,	Ortley,
Tompkins King,	Red Canada,
Wagener,	R. I. Greening,
Wealthy,	St. Lawrence,
Yellow Transparent.	Smokehouse,
	Twenty Ounce,
	Willow Twig,
	Winter Pearmain.

The list below was prepared from notes taken in 1906 when apple blight was more prevalent in western New York than ever before known. Only well known varieties are listed. Sorts intermediate to blight are not listed.

SUSCEPTIBILITY OF APPLES TO APPLE BLIGHT.

Immune in 1906.	*Very susceptible.*
Babbitt,	Alexander,
Baldwin,	Arabka,
Cox Orange,	Bailey Sweet,
Cranberry Pippin,	Bismarck,
Delicious,	Black Gilliflower,
Gideon,	Constantine,
Grimes,	Esopus *Spitzenburg*,
Lady,	Fall Pippin,
Northern Spy,	Jonathan,
Swaar,	Mother,
Sweet Bough,	Pewaukee,
Tompkins King,	Ralls,
Twenty Ounce,	R. I. Greening,
Wagener,	Rome,
Washington Strawberry.	Sutton.

There is another form of natural resistance to disease, too often neglected by plant pathologists and plant-growers alike, which is too important to let pass without a word. This is the resistance made by strong, able-bodied, well-fed, healthy, vigorous plants. Any and all of the things that contribute to highest vigor in a plant add to its capacity to resist or throw off disease and the reverse condition predisposes to the contraction of disease. There is no experimental evidence in confirmation of the statement just made but it has so much observational foundation that it may be put in positive words.

SEEDLESS APPLES.

Periodically the imagination of fruit-growers is excited by reports of new and wonderful seedless apples. But as yet, the seedless apple is a chimera from the standpoint of utility. The fruits are usually very deficient in size, color or quality — the latter in particular. Most of them are also abnormal in other respects than in fewness of seeds. In many varieties of apples seedless individuals are now and then found. On the other hand there seems to be no known case in which all of the apples in seedless varieties are lacking in seeds.

Seedless apples are not new. They were known to the Greeks [1] and the Romans. They have been described time and time again since Pliny [2] wrote of Roman agriculture. Descriptions of these outbreaks of Nature's usually orderly course are so common in both botanical and horticultural books that there is no need to repeat them even to the general public who scarcely more than yesterday had dinned into their ears tales of a marvelous seedless apple which led to a full discussion of the whole subject. The commercial history of the apple just referred to was so unsavory that it would seem wisest to keep discreetly silent on this subject for some time to come. But fruit-growers, even those to whom the seedless apple is a sore point, can bear the statement of a few facts.

Seedlessness is a permanent and a valuable character in many fruits. Thus, there are seedless varieties of the banana, barberry,

---

[1] Theophrastus. De caus. pi. Lib. 3, c. 23.
[2] Pliny. Lib. XV, c. 15.

breadfruit, date, persimmon, fig, grape, lemon, medlar, mulberry, opuntia, orange, peach, pear, pineapple, pistacio, plum, pomegranate, and strawberry. In several of these fruits seedlessness is a commercial asset. A variety of apples without seeds, especially if it were coreless as well, attractive in appearance and of high quality, would all but revolutionize apple-growing. Here, then, is a chance for the plant-breeder to exercise his art.

Seedlessness in the fruits named,— many other illustrations might be given from vegetable, flower and field crops,— establishes the fact that the production of seed is not necessary for the health and vigor of plants; and in plants propagated vegetatively seeds are useless, cumbersome organs. The sooner we get rid of seeds and cores in apples the better; and given time and patience it can be done,— indeed, has been done, but the barrenness did not occur in conjunction with other desirable qualities.

What means may the fruit-grower employ to obtain seedless apples? This is the important question. We might breed seedless apples more intelligently if we knew precisely what causes the suppression of seeds. Seedless apples seem to be produced under several conditions. Thus, this fruit is reported to be usually seedless when grown in semi-tropic countries and under other conditions which cause very luxuriant growth. This antagonism between growth and seed-production is not, however, capable of being transmitted either through seeds or buds. Hybridization is a well-known agent in diminishing the number, size and fertility of seeds in plants when the cross is a violent one or between distinct species. But crossing varieties of apples, so far as the experience at this Station goes or the scant and fragmentary accounts in literature show, has little effect on seed-bearing. Seedless apples and pears have been produced by Ewert, a German, at will, by protecting the stigmas from pollen. But none nor all of these causes acting alone or in combination for a short period nor accumulatively over a long one seem to account satisfactorily for seedless fruits.

Seedless varieties usually bear abnormal flowers, these either lacking sexual organs or petals or both. So marked are these monstrosities that the varieties are usually said to be " bloomless " as well as "seedless." Now this suppression of floral organs and seeds comes from seedlings, so far as we can learn from the more or less obscure histories of a score of seedless apples, from normal parents. In no case is there anything to lead to the suspicion that the loss of the capacity to produce seeds is the accumulated retrogression of several generations. In other words, seedless varieties of apples, and of such other fruits as opportunity has offered to study, appear to be sports or mutations. The Navel orange, the Stoneless plum, the Lombardy poplar, Sultana, Zante and several other grapes are well known varieties of species which commonly bear seeds. All historical evidence shows that these probably came into being as mutations.

Curiously enough no one seems ever to have tried planting the occasional seed to be found in seedless fruits, thus to ascertain whether the abnormality is passed from parent to offspring. If true mutations, such should be the case. Seedlings of seedless apples and a seedless pear, though crossed with other varieties, should fruit at Geneva this year or next and in time we may know more about the inheritance of seedlessness. Meanwhile, apple-growers everywhere should be on the lookout for seedless sorts and when found, even though other characters are such as to make them worthless, they should be preserved as possible starting points for new and better seedless kinds if hybridization be possible or if they can be made to produce a few selfed seeds.

A character so markedly abnormal as seedlessness might be expected to carry with it correlations in fruit or plant. In the observation of seedlessness at this Station the search for correlations has been fascinating, indeed irresistible, but the rewards have been no greater than in similar searches for this interesting phenomenon — correlation. A few dubious statements can be set down from the hasty work done with the apples on our grounds. The abortion or malformation of one or several of the floral organs that accompanies most of the seedless apples has been mentioned. Such abnormalities are, of course, cause of the effect more than correlations with seedlessness. The apples in all seedless varieties that we have seen are below medium in size, showing a tendency to decrease in size with seedlessness. The varieties are usually productive — at least there is nothing to indicate incompatibility between seedlessness and fruitfulness. The flavor of all of these seedless apples is below the mark, probably through accident. The cores are usually small and partly or, in a few cases, wholly absent.

These brief statements serve to introduce a list of growers of different varieties of seedless apples reported in the United States during the past twenty years, with the place of origin. There are probably a few duplications in this list and it is certain that it is not complete. Many of the men named do not respond to letters, but an investigation would probably lead to the discovery that the seedless variety is still in existence in the locality. Trees from those marked with an asterisk are under cultivation on our grounds. We shall be glad to have cions or buds of other seedless sorts with the hope that from some existing seedless apple may be bred a worthy variety without seeds.

Atlas J. Allen, Waynesville, N. C.,
J. H. Bailey, Linn, W. Va.,
H. E. Bemis, Green Cove Springs, Fla.,
Miss Portia E. Binkerd, West Monterey, Pa.,
T. J. F. Browns, Sands, N. C.,
Benj. Buckman, Farmingdale, Ill.,
W. M. Burns, Grantville, W. Va.,
Thos. P. Butcher, Parkersburg, W. Va.,
C. O. Crosby, Coquille, Ore.,
Samuel Donaldson, Kittanning, Pa.,
F. B. Doran, Clarkson, Va.,
*Fairbury Nurseries, Fairbury, Neb.,
James Flury, Lindsey, Ont.,
H. H. Farthing, Hattie, N. C.,
E. O. Goff, Spencer, W. Va.,
E. S. Granel, Cleveland, Ohio,
W. H. Hart, Arlington, N. Y.,
C. F. Hodge, Worcester, Mass.,
C. S. Hunter, Seven Mile, Ohio,
Dr. Nannestad B. Jorn, Brooklyn, N. Y.,

W. T. Macoun, Ottawa, Canada,
W. S. Miller, Martinsburg, W. Va.,
*D. J. Miller, Millersburg, Ohio,
Geo. E. Murrell, Fontella, Va.,
Geo. Peters & Co., Troy, Ohio,
A. J. Reaser, Roncerverte, W. Va.,
Mrs. J. P. Reichert, Manorville, Pa.,
G. W. Robinette, Flag Pond, Va.,
E. L. Smith, Hood River, Ore.,
*J. F. Spencer, Grand Junction, Colo.,
G. W. Stewart, Newport, Me.,
*Dept. No. 24476 — Van Hoy Seedless,
*Dept. No. 24626 — No Blow Seedless,
*Dept. No. 40830 — Bloomless & Seedless,
*Dept. No. 40833 — Parker Seedless,
} U. S. D. A.,
J. Van Lindley, Pomona, N. C.,
Chas. L. Wayland, Crozet, Va.,
*Chas. Waters, Bingen, Wash.,
*Edward Wellington, Waltham, Mass.

CATALOG OF APPLES.

This catalog contains 804 apples. The majority of these, 698 in all, were described in the Apples of New York[1] and in Bulletin 275[2] from this Station. Nearly all of the varieties found in the three publications are, or have been, grown in the Station orchard. Some changes have been made in the discussion of the old varieties and the Station records of new varieties have been supplemented by information from originators and introducers. To enable fruit-growers to dig a little below the surface in using the catalog a few explanatory notes are necessary.

Place of origin.— The first column in the catalog gives the place of origin of the varieties. The origin of a fruit is well worth knowing for its practical value, as it often helps very materially in determining whether a variety should be planted in a region. Thus, it may be assumed that the Russian sorts grown in America are particularly well suited to northern regions; that those from south of the Mason and Dixon line are true southerners as those from the north are northerners; it may even be assumed that an apple originating in New York will succeed there better than in any adjoining State, as it must have been well fitted to its habitat to have succeeded well enough to get out of the limbo of unnamed seedlings. To this statement there are several notable exceptions, some sorts thriving within the State that according to theory ought to fail forthwith.

Bearing age.— The second column tells the number of years it took varieties to come into bearing in the Station orchard. The ages of bearing are not very trustworthy; for in most cases there have been but two trees and the varieties were not planted the same year. And, again, a decade or more ago when trees were headed high and pruned much, it took them longer to come into bearing than nowadays when we head low and prune little. Yet the ages given are suggestive and seem to the authors worth printing.

---

[1] N. Y. Agr. Exp. Sta. "Apples of New York."
[2] N. Y. Agr. Exp. Sta. Bull. 275.

Form.—The third column gives the form of fruit in varieties. An especial attempt has been made to make as accurate a pen picture of the form of apples as can be made in an abbreviated description under the belief that form as compared with size and color in giving apples handsome appearance is usually underrated. The mould in which it is cast very often determines the attractiveness of an apple to the prospective consumer. To use this catalog intelligently, then, the reader must have in his mind the exact form for which each abbreviation in the third column stands.

Size.— In the fourth column the size of varieties is indicated. In the eye of the average person, size is esteemed about the highest quality a fruit may possess. Large size is distinctly meritorious in culinary apples, saving waste in paring and coring, but for dessert the medium sized fruit should be preferred — mere size is about the least needed quality. This distinction between culinary and dessert apples should be kept in mind in using this catalog. It should be remembered, too, that quality is in no way correlated with size in a variety though it may be in individuals, as when undue size has been brought about by irrigation, rich soil, or girdling, in all of which cases large size is accompanied by low quality.

Color.— The abbreviations in column five give as accurately as possible the color of varieties. This character is of utmost importance in identifying varieties but does not, as many appear to think, indicate in the least the quality of the fruit — color and quality are not correlated. Connoisseurs find yellow, green or russet apples quite as high in quality as the red sorts. The average person, personification of the consumer, makes a fetish of red, the more brilliant the better, and this must be taken in account in choosing color, paradoxical though it is that while apples are grown to eat we grow that which is scarcely fit to eat provided only that it have brilliant color. In studying this character, keep in mind that color is much influenced by environment, especially by soil and sunshine.

Color of flesh.— This character is of very great importance in identifying some varieties. There are, as column six shows, but few colors; but these are distinctive, as permanent as almost any other character of the apple and are plainly indicated by the abbreviations. Color of flesh, as with color of skin, gives no clue to quality in varieties.

Flavor.—Under flavor, as described in the seventh column, the degree of sweetness and acidity of a variety is described by terms which need no defining. Flavor is a concrete and definite part of quality and should be noted, therefore, in connection with the descriptions of quality as given in the next column.

Quality.— That undefined thing known as quality is set forth in the eighth column. What is quality? The word is constantly rolled under the tongue by growers and consumers but like good cheer in the fable is fish to one, flesh to another and fowl to a third. As used in this catalog we mean, in brief, that combination of flavor, aroma, juiciness and tender flesh which makes an apple agreeable to the palate. Beside these there is a wholly undefinable thing in the quality of a fruit which in human beings would be called personality. Some apples, as the McIntosh, Spy, Spitzenburg, Newtown Pippin or Grimes — and all sorts of high quality — have this individuality which separates them from commonplace sorts. It is quite impossible for one person to convey to another in a column of abbreviations the flavor, aroma, juiciness, tenderness and "personality" of a variety of apples. All that the authors can do is to express the degree of goodness of quality as it appeals to their tastes by such simple words as best, good, fair, poor, with the adverb "very" now and then used to still further separate the degree.

Use.—In the ninth column the use is denominated. The use has been arbitrarily determined by the describers. If an apple is choicely good, it is put down as a "dessert" sort; if not especially pleasing to the taste it is roughly lumped as a "kitchen" apple. This is not fair to the kitchen but this is the method of separation everywhere in vogue. Some sorts are marked for both dessert and kitchen; most of these have been tried or prepared in one or more ways for the table. It may usually be assumed, but not always, that a good dessert apple is a good kitchen apple. A dessert apple may always be considered valuable for home use. Desirability for cider or for local, general or foreign markets is designated only under " remarks."

Season.—The tenth column shows the season of varieties. The data regarding keeping quality has been taken from apples in common storage and covers periods of from one to ten seasons. The amount of fruit stored ranges from a peck to a bushel, the aim being to put in storage each year a bushel of each variety for the long-keeping test. The months given are those in which the apples become edible and in which they pass entirely out of season — a very wide range for which allowance must be made.

Apple regions of New York.—The next nine columns list apples for the nine pomological regions into which New York may be divided. The lists are founded upon the reputed behavior of the varieties in the regions as to size, color, keeping quality, and flavor of fruit; and as to longevity, vigor, health and productiveness of tree. In some cases varieties have been put in the list for a region because of its reputation as to the characters named in an adjoining or similar region.

The pomological regions of New York have been set off somewhat in accordance with the physical geography of the State but more particularly with reference to the distribution of its wild and domesticated plants. Not much attention could be paid to soils, since through glacial action these have been carried to and fro so that there are few large areas in the State in which there is any great degree of uniformity. It must not be thought, however, that soils are not important determinants of profitable fruit-growing; to the contrary, they set the seal of profit of kind and of variety of fruit and must ever be considered.

The following are the nine pomological regions of New York:

Long Island.— This district is composed of the sandy lowland of Long Island. It is a low plain covered with a thick deposit in which sand predominates. The varieties of fruits cultivated here, and especially of the apple, are not very distinctive. The limits of the northern and of southern sorts meet, giving a great number of varieties for the district and making it difficult to form a definite list.

Hudson Valley.— This region lies on both sides of the Hudson from Long Island to the valley of Lake George in Warren and Washington counties. The varied topography and the several geological formations giving different soils make it possible, and probably desirable, to subdivide this district into several secondary regions. But the district is considered as one in the horticultural literature of the State; our data have been collected for the united district; and since it would complicate the work of making out lists very greatly, subdivisions have not been made.

The complexities of climate, topography and soil, however, must be kept in mind in using the table of adaptations. Where the region touches the seashore, and for several miles inland, the list prepared for Long Island will be applicable. In the northern part of the region and the high altitudes the varieties recommended for the Champlain valley should all thrive.

St. Lawrence and Champlain valleys.— This region is the high and rolling land tributary to Lake Champlain and the St. Lawrence river and such parts of the Adirondacks as are adapted to apple-growing. Three divisions could well be made of this district; the two valleys could be kept distinct, each to include only the area of lower land adjacent to the water; and the third to be the high uplands which run back into the Adirondacks. We have no data, however, which indicate that lists for the three districts would differ greatly and we have therefore included them as one. It is hardly necessary to say that only the hardiest varieties would thrive in the high uplands and that in favored locations near the water some of the more southern and more tender sorts could be grown.

Mohawk Valley.—The valley of the Mohawk from Oneida Lake to the valley of the Hudson is a district of indistinct boundaries and possibly should be divided into the Upper Mohawk and the Lower Mohawk districts, in which case the Lower Mohawk could include the Schoharie valley, where some fruits succeed remarkably well. A fruit list for the Lower Mohawk would include sorts recommended for the Hudson valley. Hardiness is a prime requisite for the Upper Mohawk, though some varieties can be grown which will not thrive in the district to the north, since the season is somewhat longer.

Eastern plateau.—The Catskills and the high plateau to the west reaching to the basin of the Central Lakes form a very distinct region. The western boundary of this region cannot be drawn with definiteness but the eastern boundary is well drawn, being the highlands overlooking the Hudson Valley. This is an agricultural rather than a pomological region and though the apple succeeds remarkably well in some valleys, apple-growing is not sufficiently well developed to furnish data for a very reliable list. The varieties named are those which succeed well under many conditions and especially in cold climates since so much of this district is high and cold.

Central Lakes.—The great basin in which lie the Central Lakes is a region of very indefinite boundaries the fruit lands of which lie for the most part in the lower and more level lands near the lakes. A glance at the list of apples will give an idea of the importance of this district in the apple industry. Unusually favorable conditions prevail in this and in the district to the north for the growth of the apple, the two comprising what is known as the Western New York apple belt — far famed for the quality and quantity of the product.

Ontario Shore.— This region is the plain along the shore of Lake Ontario from the valley of the St. Lawrence to the Niagara river, extending from the lake on the north a distance of several miles inland to an escarpment of limestone in the neighborhood of 600 feet in height. The plain is broken up by a series of parallel hills — the drumlins of the geologists. It differs from the preceding district chiefly in the matter of soils. Several distinct types of soils to be found in the Ontario Shore district seem to be well suited to the apple. Much of the soil is sandy or loamy and is easily drained and worked. Soil and climatic conditions are such that the apple trees are exceptionally large, very productive and unusually long-lived and bear fruit of most excellent quality.

Erie Shore.— The plain along the shore of Lake Erie from the Niagara river to the western boundary of the State forms the Erie Shore district. It is a very narrow strip of land bounded on the south by a high escarpment from which it gradually descends to the lake level on the north. This district is largely given up to grape-growing, there being so few apples that it has been exceedingly difficult to secure sufficient data from which to form a list of apples.

Western Plateau.— The high plateau to the south of the Ontario and Erie shores and west of the Central Lakes is called the Western Plateau. This, like the Eastern Plateau, is a region of indefinite boundaries, varied topography, and relatively of smaller importance in the apple industry than the neighboring districts. Here again it has been difficult to get sufficient data upon which to base a list and it has been necessary to be guided in including or excluding some varieties by their behavior in other districts where conditions are much the same.

ABBREVIATIONS.— *Size.*— l, large; m, medium; s, small; v, very. *Form.*— a, angular; c, conical; l, light; r, red; ru, russet; s, striped; w, white; y, yellow. *Flavor.*— a, acid; b, brisk; m, mild; s, sweet; *Starring.*— *, recommended; **, well recommended; +, worthy of trial.

No.	VARIETY.	Origin.	Bearing age.	Form.	Size.	Color of skin.	Color of flesh.	Flavor.	Quality.	Use.	Season.
1	Adirondack	N. Y.		r c	m	y r s	y w	m sa	g	k	Oct., Jan.
2	Admirable	Eng.		r o c	m	g y	y w	m sa	g–vg	d	Oct., Jan.
3	Akin	Ill.	8 yrs.	r o i	m	y r s	y	b sa	g	d	Jan., June
4	Alabama	Unk.		r i	m	y g r s	y	sa	f	k	Oct.
5	Albion	Unk.		r ob	l—vl	y g	y	m sa	g	d	Oct., Jan.
6	Alden	Wis.		r c	m—l	y r	y	sa	f	d	Aug., Sept.
7	Alexander	Rus.		r o c	vl	y r s	y w	m sa	f—g	k	Sept., Nov.
8	(II) Allington	Eng.	4 yrs.	r i	m—l	g y r s c	y	b sa	g	d k	Nov., Jan.
9	Allison	Tenn.		r o c a	m	g r s	g y	m sa	f	k	Mar., May
10	Alice	Vt.		r ob c	m	g y b	y w	s	g	k	Aug., Sept.
11	Amassia	Eu.		r c	m	y g r s	w	m sa	g—vg	d	Dec., Apr.
12	American Best	Unk.		r c	m	y b	w	m sa	g	k	Aug.
13	American Codling	Minn.?		r o c	m	g y b	y w	sa	g	k	Sept., Oct.
14	American Pippin	Unk.		o	m	g r s	y w	m sa	p—g	k	May
15	Amos	Unk.		r o	m—s	y b	y w	b sa	f—g	k	Nov., Mar.
16	Amsterdam	N. Y.		r o	m	g y r s	w	s	g	d	Oct., Nov.
17	Ananarnoe	Rus.		r o	m	y r s	w	sa	g	k	Sept.
18	Andrews Winter	Unk.		r c	s	y g r s	w	m sa	f—g	d	Mar., June
19	Angers	Unk.		r c	l	g y r	y	b sa	g	k	Nov., Dec.
20	Anisim	Rus.		r c	m—s	g y r	g w	m sa	g	d	Oct., Dec.
21	Anis Rose	Rus.		r o	m—l	y w r s	w	sa	g	k	Aug., Sept.
22	Antonovka	Rus.		r	l	y	y	b sa	g	k	Oct.
23	Aport Orient	Rus.		r ob c	l	y r s	y w	m sa	f	k	Aug.
24	Arabka	Rus.	6 yrs.	r o	l—vl	g y b d	w	b sa	f	k	Nov., Dec.
25	Arctic	N. Y.		r o c	l—m	y r s	y	m sa	g	k	Oct., Feb.
26	Arkansas	Ark.	8 yrs.	r c	l—m	g y r s	g w	sa	g	k	Dec., May
27	Arkansas Beauty	Ark.	8 yrs.	r c	m—l	g y r s	y w	m sa	g	k	Jan., Feb.
28	Arkansas Black	Ark.		r	m	y d r	y	b sa	g	k	Dec., Apr.
29	Armorel	Eu.	4 yrs.	o	s	y ru	y	b sa	g	k	Jan., Mar.
30	Arnold	Can.		o	m	y w b	y	m sa	v g	d	Nov., Mar.
31	Arthur	Ia.		ob	m—s	y g r s	y	sa	f—g	k	Oct., Jan.
32	Aucuba	Fr.		r c	m	y r s	y w	b sa	g—vg	k	Oct., Jan.
33	August	Minn.		r o c	m—s	g y r s	y	m sa	f	k	Aug., Sept.
34	Augustine	Va.?		r ob c	m—l	y r s	....	s	g	d	Aug.
35	Autumn Bough	Am.		ob c	l	y	w	s	vg	d k	Aug., Sept.
36	Autumn Streaked	Rus.		r o	l	y r s	y	sa	g	k	Sept.
37	Autumn Swaar	Unk.		r o c	m—l	g y	y	m sa	vg	d k	Sept.
38	Autumn Sweet Swaar	Unk.		r o	l	y	y w	v s	vg—b	d	Sept., Oct.
39	Avery	Unk.		r o c	l	g y r s c	y	b sa	f	k	Sept., Oct.
40	Axident	Kan.		r c	l	y d r c	y	sa	g	d k	Jan., Mar.
41	Babbitt	Ill.	11 yrs.	r o	l	y r s		b sa	g	k	Nov., Feb.
42	Bailey Spice	N. Y.		r c	m	y	w	sa	g—vg	d	Sept., Oct.
43	Bailey *Sweet*	N. Y.	8 yrs.	r c	l—m	y r s	y	s	vg	d k	Oct., Jan.
44	Baker	Conn.		r c	m—l	y g r s	y	m sa	g	k	Oct., Feb.
45	Baker Sweet	Conn.	10 yrs.	r	m	y	y	s	g—vg	d	Nov., Dec.
46	Baldwin	Mass.	8 yrs.	r c	l	y r s	y	b sa	g—vg	d k	Nov., Mar.
47	Banana Sweet	N. J.		r c	l	g y b	w	s	g	d k	Jan., Mar.
48	Banks	A bud sport of Gravenstein, much higher colored than that variety.									
49	Baptist	Ky.		o r	m—s	g y r s	y	m sa	f—g	d	Jan., June
50	Barbel	Rus.		o c	m—l	y r	y	sa	g	d	Oct., Feb.
51	Barcroft	Pa.		r o	s	g y b	....	m sa	g	k	Dec.
52	Barnes Choice	Unk.		r o	s—m	g y b	w	b sa	g	k	Sept.
53	Barringer	N. Y.		r c	l—m	r s	y w	m sa	vg	d	Dec., Mar.
54	Barry	N. Y.		r o	m—l	y b	y w	b sa	g	k	Nov., Dec.
55	Barton	N. Y.		r o	l	y r s c	y w	m sa	f	d	Sept., Oct.
56	Battyani	Eu.		r o c	l	g y d b	y w	b sa	g	k	Dec., Jan.
57	Batullen	Eu.		r c	m	g y	y	sa	vg	d	Nov., Mar.
58	Baxter	Can.		r c	l—vl	y r s	y	m sa	f—g	k	Nov., Jan.
59	Bayard	Unk.		o c	l	y d r c	y w	sa	f	k	Nov., Dec.

i, irregular; o, oblate; ob, oblong; ov, ovate; r, roundish.   *Color.*— b, blush; c, carmine; d, dark; g, green; sa, subacid.   *Quality.*— b, best; g, good; f, fair; p, poor; v, very.   *Use.*— d, dessert; k, kitchen.

No.	Long Island.	Hudson Valley.	St. Lawrence and Champlain Vl'ys.	Mohawk Valley.	Eastern Plateau.	Central Lakes.	Ontario Shore.	Erie Shore.	Western Plateau.	REMARKS.
1										Promising early winter apple for northern New York.
2										Not recommended for New York.
3	+	+				+				A beautiful apple of good quality.
4										Not recommended.
5										Surpassed by others of its season.
6										Not valuable.
7	*	*	**	**		**	**	**	*	Tree characters good. Fruit large and beautiful but of only fair quality. A commercial variety.
8										An English variety not valuable in New York.
9										A Southern apple not promising in New York.
10										Discarded at this Station.
11										A European variety of no value.
12										Of no value.
13										Of no value.
14										Probably two varieties under this name. Neither valuable.
15										A Southern variety worthless in New York.
16										Not valuable.
17										Not desirable.
18										Worthless.
19										Of no value.
20										May be of value where superior hardiness is a prime requisite.
21	+	+	+	+	+	+	+	+	+	Worthy of testing.
22										Of no value.
23										Not recommended for New York.
24										Worthless in New York.
25			*	*						Worthy of trial in northern New York.
26										Valuable in the South but not in New York.
27										Not valuable.
28										Not valuable in New York.
29										Not recommended.
30										A Northern Spy seedling. Too tender for market.
31										A Northwestern variety nearly as hardy as Oldenburg.
32										A French apple of doubtful value here.
33										Not recommended.
34										Discarded.
35	*	*		*	*	*	*	*	*	Ranks among our best sweet apples.
36										Somewhat like the Oldenburg but surpassed by that variety.
37										Hardy and vigorous but lacks productiveness.
38										Crowded out by better sorts of its season.
39										Worthless.
40										Hardly worth planting.
41										A shy bearer.
42										Now nearly obsolete.
43										Fruit of fine appearance. Tree characters undesirable.
44										An old variety superseded by the Baldwin. Nearly obsolete.
45										An old variety, productive. No commercial importance.
46	**	**	**	**	**	**	**	**	**	Standard winter apple of New York.
47										Little known in New York.
48	+	+	+	+	+	+	+	+	+	
49										Fruit very inferior.
50										A hardy tree bearing rather inferior fruit.
51										Of no value.
52										Not recommended.
53										A local apple known only in Columbia county.
54										Not valuable.
55										Of no value.
56										Surpassed by better varieties.
57										Unproductive at this Station.
58			**	*						Valuable in northern New York.
59										Not recommended.

ABBREVIATIONS.— *Size.*— l, large; m, medium; s, small; v, very. *Form.*— a, angular; c, conical; l, light; r, red; ru, russet; s, striped; w, white; y, yellow. *Flavor.*— a, acid; b, brisk; m, mild; s, sweet; *Starring.*— *, recommended; **, well recommended; +, worthy of trial.

No.	VARIETY.	Origin.	Bearing age.	Form.	Size.	Color of skin.	Color of flesh.	Flavor.	Quality.	Use.	Season.
60	Beach	Ark	7 yrs.	r	m	y r s	y w	sa	f—g	k	Feb., May
61	Beautiful Arcad	Rus		o b	m	y r s		s	vg	d	Aug., Sept.
62	Beauty of Bath	Eng.?	7 yrs.	o	m	y r s c	y w	sa	g	d	Aug.
63	Beauty of Kent	Eng		r	l	g y r s	y	sa	g	k	Oct., Nov.
64	Belborodooskoe	Rus	8 yrs.	r	m—l	g y	w	m sa	g	k	Aug.
65	Belle et Bonne	Eu		r o	l—vl	y g	y	m sa	g	k	Nov., Jan.
66	Belmont	Pa		r ob c	m—l	y b	y	m sa	vg	k d	Oct., Feb.
67	Ben Davis	Ky	4 yrs.	r ob c	m—l	y r s	w y	m sa	g	k	Jan., June
68	Ben Hur	Ind		r ob c	l	g y r s c	y w	m sa	f—g	k	Dec., Feb.
69	Benninger	Pa	6 yrs.	r o	m	y r s	y	m sa	g	d	Aug., Sept.
70	Benoni	Mass		r c	m	y r s	y	sa	g—vg	k	Aug., Sept.
71	Bentley	Va. ?		r ob c	m	y r s	w	s	g	k	Dec., May
72	Bergen	N. Y		r	m	g w r s	w	m sa	g	k d	Jan., Feb.
73	Bess Pool	Eng		r c	m	y r s	w	b sa	g	d k	Nov., Mar.
74	Bethel	Vt		r c	l	y r s	w	m sa	f—g	k d	Nov., Mar.
75	Bethlehemite	O. ?		r o c	m	y g r s	w	m sa	g—vg	d k	Nov., Mar.
76	Bietigheimer	Ger	8 yrs.	r o c	vl	y r s	w	sa	f—g	k	Sept., Oct.
77	Billy Bond	Eu. ?		r ob c	l—m	y r s	y	sa	g	k	Nov., Jan.
78	Birth	Rus		r c	m—l	g y b	w	m sa	f	k	Sept.
79	Bismarck	N. Z	7 yrs.	r o c	l—vl	y r s	w	sa	f—g	k	Oct., Dec.
80	Black Annette	N. E. ?		r o	m	g d r s	w	m sa	vg	d	Dec., Apr.
81	Black Ben Davis	Ark	5 yrs.	r c	m—l	y d r	w	m sa	g	k	Jan., Apr.
82	Black Gilliflower	Am	12 yrs.	ob c	m—l	y g d r	w	m sa	g	d k	Oct., Feb.
83	Blenheim	Eng		r o c	l—m	y r	y w	m sa	g—vg	d k	Oct., Dec.
84	Blood Red	Minn		o	m	y r	y	m sa	g	k	Sept., Oct.
85	Bloomfield	Md		r o c	l—m	y g r	y	sa	f	k	Oct., Nov.
86	Blue Pearmain	Unk		r	l—m	y d r s	y	m sa	g	d k	Oct., Mar.
87	Blushed Calville	Rus		r c	m—l	y g b r	w	sa	f—g	k	Aug.
88	Blushing Bride	Unk		r o c	m—s	y d r	y g	m sa	f	k	Nov., Dec.
89	Bogdanoff Glass	Rus	8 yrs.	r c	l	g y b	g w	b sa	f—g	k	Nov., Feb.
90	Boiken	Eu	5 yrs.	o c a	m—vl	y b	w	b sa	g	k	Nov., Mar.
91	Bonum	N. C		o	m—l	y r s	y w	m sa	v g	d k	Nov., Dec.
92	Borovinka	Rus	7 yrs.	r	m—l	y r s	y	sa	g	k	Aug., Sept.
93	Borsdorf	Ger		o	m—s	y b	w	m sa	f	k	Nov., Feb.
94	Boskoop	Eu		o		y g r	y	b sa	g	k	Sept., Nov.
95	Bostick	Unk	9 yrs.	r o c	l	y r s c	y w	m sa	f	k	Nov., Dec.
96	Boston Russet	N. Y		r c	m	y g ru	y	m sa	f—g	k	Jan., Apr.
97	Bottle Greening	Vt		r o c	m—l	g y b	y w	sa	g—vg	d k	Oct., Mar.
98	Boy's Delight	Can		r	m	g y r s	w	m sa	g	d	Oct., Jan.
99	Brackett	Am		o	m	g b d r	y w	sa	p	k	Jan., Apr.
100	Bramley	Eu	6 yrs.	r o	l	y g r s c	w	b sa	g	k	Nov., Dec.
101	Breskovka	Rus	6 yrs.	r	m	y	w	sa	f—g	k	Aug., Sept.
102	Brown	Unk		r o	m—l	y g b	y	sa	g	k	Sept.
103	Brownlees	Eng		o	m—l	y ru	y w	b sa	vg	d k	Oct., Jan.
104	Brown Sweet	N. Y		ob c	l	g y b	y	s	g—vg	d k	Sept., Jan.
105	Buckingham	Am		o	l	y g r s	y	m sa	f—g	k	Nov., Apr.
106	Buda	Unk		r o c	l	g y r s c	y w	sa	f—g	k	Sept.
107	Bullock	N. J		r c	m	y g ru	y	m sa	vg—b	d	Oct., Jan.
108	Bunker Hill	N. Y		r c	m	y r s	w	sa	vg	d	Oct.
109	Butter	Pa		r	m	y	w	s	g—vg	k	Sept., Oct.
110	Cabashea	N. Y		r o	l—vl	y g r s	y	b sa	g	k d	Sept., Oct.
111	Cagle	Unk		r o c	s	y g d r s	w y	sa	f	k	Mar., Apr.
112	Calville de Oullins	Unk		r c	m—l	y r s	y	sa	f	k	Jan., Apr.
113	Campfield	N. J		r o	m—l	y r s	w	s	g	k	Dec., May
114	Canada Baldwin	Can		r o c	m	y g r s	w	m sa	g—vg	d	Nov., Jan.
115	Canada Reinette	Unk		r o c	m—l	y b	y	sa	vg	d k	Dec., Apr.
116	Cannon *Pearmain*	Am		r o v	m—l	g y r s	y	sa	g	k	Jan., Apr
117	Carlough	N. Y		r c	m—l	g y b	w	m sa	g	d k	Nov., Apr

i, irregular; o, oblate; ob, oblong; ov, ovate; r, roundish.   *Color.*— b, blush; c, carmine; d, dark; g, green; sa, subacid.   *Quality.*— b, best; g, good; f, fair; p, poor; v, very.   *Use.*— d, dessert; k, kitchen.

No.	Long Island.	Hudson Valley.	St. Lawrence and Champlain Vl'ys.	Mohawk Valley.	Eastern Plateau.	Central Lakes.	Ontario Shore.	Erie Shore.	Western Plateau.	REMARKS.
60										Not promising in this State.
61										Not recommended.
62										Might be valuable for home use.
63										Of no value.
64										Not worthy of attention in this State.
65										An old variety not equal to standard kinds.
66										Valuable for home orchards only.
67	**	**				**	**	**		Hardy, healthy, vigorous, productive. Lacks quality.
68										A Rome-Ben Davis cross. Not fully tested.
69										A pleasant flavored apple.
70										Attractive, excellent, but not large enough for market.
71										Not valuable.
72										A local variety of no importance.
73										An English variety. Poor cropper in New York.
74			**							Blue Pearmain type. Valuable in northeastern New York.
75										Newtown Spitzenburg type but surpassed by that variety.
76										Suitable for exhibition purposes only.
77										Tree characters good. Inferior in quality. Of questionable value.
78										Of no value.
79	*	*	**	*	*	*	*	*	*	Tree hardy, healthy; bears young and productive. Fruit attractive but inferior in quality.
80										Has proved very hardy in the Northwest.
81	**	**				**	**	**		Ben Davis type, and of value.
82	**	**				**	**	**		An old but still valuable variety.
83										Fruit is desirable, but tree characters are unsatisfactory.
84										Not worth planting.
85										Attractive in appearance but surpassed by other varieties.
86										An old variety now rarely planted.
87										Of no value.
88										Not recommended.
89										Hardy. May have some value in northern regions.
90		*	*	*	*	*		*	*	Widely planted as a filler, but not very desirable.
91										Not adapted to this latitude.
92										Resembles Oldenburg and surpassed by it.
93										Not recommended.
94										Quality inferior. Not worthy of planting.
95										Not adapted to this latitude.
96										Grown only about Albion, N. Y.; not valuable.
97										Tree characters good and quality high. Poor shipper.
98										A Fameuse seedling not as good as McIntosh.
99										Worthless for commercial planting.
100										Of no value. Surpassed by other varieties.
101										Not recommended.
102										Not worth planting.
103										Excellent, but lacks productiveness.
104										An Oswego county variety as yet untested elsewhere.
105										A southern apple not recommended for New York.
106										Of no value commercially.
107										High quality; small; tree characters poor.
108										Not known outside of central New York.
109										Probably not know in New York.
110										Trees unproductive, fruit unattractive.
111										Worthless.
112										Not recommended.
113										An old cider apple now practically obsolete.
114										Fameuse type. Later than Fameuse; not desirable.
115										Excelled by other varieties.
116										Valued in the South. Not adapted to New York conditions.
117										Of doubtful value in New York.

ABBREVIATIONS.— *Size.*— l, large; m, medium; s, small; v, very. *Form.*— a, angular; c, conical; l, light; r, red; ru, russet; s, striped; w, white; y, yellow. *Flavor.*— a, acid; b, brisk; m, mild; s, sweet; *Starring.*— *, recommended; **, well recommended; +, worthy of trial.

No.	VARIETY.	Origin.	Bearing age.	Form.	Size.	Color of skin.	Color of flesh.	Flavor.	Quality.	Use.	Season.
118	Carpentin	Unk		r c	s—vs	r ru	w	b sa	vg	d	Dec., Apr.
119	Cathead	Eu		r	vl	g	y w	sa	g	k	Oct., Nov.
120	Caywood	N. Y		o	m	y b	y	m sa	g	d	Jan., Apr.
121	Celestia	O		r c	m—l	g y b	y	m sa	g	d	Oct., Jan.
122	Centennial	Unk		r c i	m	y r s c	w	sa	f	k	Oct.
123	Challenger	Unk	8 yrs.	r c	m	g y r	y	s	f	k	Dec., Apr.
124	Champaign	Rus		r o	m	g y r s c	w	sa	f	k	July, Aug.
125	Champlain	Vt. ?		r c	m—l	g y b	w	m sa	g—vg	k d	Aug., Oct.
126	Chandler	Am		r o	l	g y r s	g w	sa	g—vg	d	Oct., Dec.
127	Charlamoff	Rus		r ob	l—m	y r s	y	sa	g	k	Aug.
128	Charlock Reinette	Rus		o	l—m	g y r s	y	sa	g	k	Sept., Oct.
129	Cheeseboro	Unk		r c	l—vl	g ru	....	m sa	f	k	Oct., Dec.
130	Chenango	N. Y		r ob c	l—m	y r s	w	m sa	g—vg	d	Aug., Sept.
131	Chicago	Ill		o	m—l	g y r c	y	m sa	f	d	Nov., Dec.
132	Clapper	N. Y		o c	m	y r s	y	sa	g	k	Sept., Oct.
133	Clarke	N. Y		r o c	m—l	g y b	w	b sa	g—vg	d	Oct., Jan.
134	Clayton	Ind		r o c	l—m	y r s	y	m sa	g	k d	Jan., May
135	Cleopatra	Unk		ob c	l	y b	y	sa	g	d	Dec., Jan.
136	Clinton	N. Y	4 yrs.	r o c	l	g y b	y	sa	g	k	Dec., Feb.
137	Clyde	N. Y		r ob c	l	g y r s	w	sa	g—vg	d k	Oct., Dec.
138	Coffelt	Ark		r o	m	y r s	g y	m sa	g	k	Jan., May
139	Cogswell	Conn		r c	m	y r s	y	m sa	f—g	d	Dec., Mar.
140	Collamer	A red strain of Twenty Ounce.									
141	Collins	Ark	7 yrs.	r o	l—m	y r s	y	sa	f—g	k	Jan., June
142	Colton	Mass		r	m	g y b	w	m sa	f—g	k	July, Sept.
143	Colvert	Am		o c	l	g y r s	y w	sa	g	k	Oct., Jan.
144	Constantine	Rus		r c	l—vl	g y r s	g w	b sa	f—g	k	Sept., Nov.
145	Cooper	Unk		r o	l	g y r s	....	sa	g	k	Oct., Dec.
146	Cooper Market	Pa	5 yrs.	r o v	m	y g r s	w	b sa	f—g	k	Jan., June
147	Cornell	Pa.?		r o c	l—m	y r s c	w	sa	vg	d	Sept. Nov.
148	Corner	N. Y		o	m—l	y r s	y	m sa	vg	d	Nov., Dec.
149	Cortland	N. Y	6 yrs.	r o	l	y d r s c	w	sa	g	d k	Nov., Feb.
150	Counseilor Niemetz	Rus		o c	m—s	y b r	y	a	f	k	Nov., Jan.
151	Count Orloff	Rus		r o c	m	g r s	w	m sa	f	k	Aug.
152	Cox Orange	Eng		r o	m	y r s	y	m sa	vg—b	d	Sept., Jan.
153	Cranberry Pippin	N. Y		r o	l	y r s	w	m sa	g	k	Oct., Feb.
154	Cream	N. Y		r o	m	y	y	s	g	d k	Sept., Oct.
155	Crimean	Rus	6 yrs.	r ob c	s	g y r s	w	sa	g	k	Sept., Oct.
156	Cross	Md		r o c	l	g w r s	w	sa	f	k	Sept., Oct.
157	Crossed No. 32	Unk		r c	m—l	g b d r	g y	sa	p	k	Dec., Jan.
158	Crotts	Kan		r ob	m—l	g r s	g y	m sa	f—g	d	Jan., May
159	Crow Egg	Ind.?		r o	m	y g	w	s	g—vg	d	Oct., Nov.
160	Crowns	Unk		r c	l	y g b	w y	b sa	g	k	Nov., Feb.
161	Czar Thorn	Rus		r c	m	g y r s	w	s	f	k	Sept.
162	Danvers *Sweet*	Mass		r c	m—l	g y b	g y	s	g—vg	d k	Nov., Apr.
163	Deacon Jones	Pa	8 yrs.	r c	l—vl	y r	y w	m sa	f—g	k	Nov., Mar.
164	Deaderick	Tenn		r c	l	g y b	y	sa	g	k	Oct., Jan.
165	De Chataigenier	Unk		o c	l	g y b	g w	m sa	f	k	Dec., Feb.
166	Delicious	Iowa	9 yrs.	r ob c	l	y r s	y	sa	g	d k	Dec., Mar.
167	Detroit Red	Am		r o c	l	y r s	w y	m sa	g—vg	d	Sept., Dec.
168	Devonshire Duke	Eng		o c	m—s	y b ry	y	sa	g—vg	d k	Dec., Apr.
169	Dickey	Ohio		o	m	y r s	y	m sa	f—g	k	Dec., Feb.
170	Dickinson	Pa		ob c	m—l	y g r s	w	sa	f—g	k	Nov., Apr.
171	Disharoon	Ga		r c	m	y g	y w	sa	g	k	Nov., Dec.
172	Doctor	Pa		o	m—l	y r s	w y	m sa	g—vg	d k	Dec., Apr.
173	Doctor Walker	Ky		r c	m	g y r s	w y	m sa	g—vg	d k	Jan., May
174	Domine	Am	5 yrs.	o	m	g y r s	w	m sa	g—vg	d k	Nov., Mar.
175	Donn Marie	N. Z.?		o	m	g b	g y	sa	f	k	Dec., Jan.
176	Double Rose	Rus		r ob c	s	y r	y	m sa	f—g	k	Nov., Feb.

i, irregular; *o*, oblate; *ob*, oblong; *ov*, ovate; *r*, roundish. *Color.*— b, blush; c, carmine; d, dark; g, green; sa, subacid. *Quality.*— b, best; g, good; f, fair; p, poor; v, very. *Use.*— d, dessert; k, kitchen.

No.	Long Island.	Hudson Valley.	St. Lawrence and Champlain Vl'ys.	Mohawk Valley.	Eastern Plateau.	Central Lakes.	Ontario Shore.	Erie Shore.	Western Plateau.	REMARKS.
118										Unique but not valuable.
119										Obsolete in New York.
120										Now practically obsolete.
121										Not recommended.
122										Not recommended.
123										A good keeper but inferior in quality. Not recommended.
124										Not recommended.
125										Tree characters good. Suitable for the home orchard.
126										Probably not known in New York.
127										Oldenburg type, but inferior to that variety.
128										Of no value.
129										An old inferior variety fast becoming obsolete.
130	**	**		**	**	**	**	**	**	Attractive, good quality, easily bruised; excellent.
131										Not recommended as a commercial variety.
132										Obsolete.
133										Known locally only.
134										A western sort not known in New York.
135										Not recommended.
136	+	+	+	+	+	+	+	+	+	Type of Green Newtown.
137										But little grown in this State.
138										Ben Davis class. Not valuable here.
139										Hardy, vigorous, unproductive. Not equal to standard sorts.
140	**	**	*	*	**	**	**	**	**	
141										May prove valuable where Ben Davis thrives.
142										Of little value.
143										Trees hardy, healthy, productive. Inferior to Twenty Ounce.
144	*	*	**	**	*	*	*	*	*	Tree and fruit characters good. Subject to blight. A market sort desirable as a filler.
145										Not recommended.
146										Hardy, productive, lacking in size and quality. Splendid keeper.
147	+	+	+	+	+	+	+	+	+	Recommended by U. S. Department of Agriculture.
148										Known locally only in Orange county.
149	+	+	+	+	+	+	+	+	+	Similar to McIntosh. Promising for commercial planting.
150										Of no value.
151										Not recommended.
152	*	*				+	+	+		Desirable for the home orchard.
153										Suitable only for the North.
154										No longer cultivated.
155										Of no value.
156										Not recommended.
157										Worthless.
158										A Rambo seedling worthless in New York.
159										Now practically obsolete.
160										Fall Pippin type but not equal to that variety.
161										Of no value.
162										Vigorous, productive. Of good size and quality, poor color.
163	+	+	+	+	+	+	+	+	+	An attractive market fruit. Heavy bearer.
164										Tree characters good but fruit inferior.
165										Of no value.
166	+	+	+	+	+	+	+	+	+	Well worth testing in New York.
167										Of Fameuse type. Surpassed by McIntosh.
168										Productive, small size, drops badly, high quality.
169										Not worthy of cultivation.
170										Poor grower, very productive. Second rate quality.
171										A Southern apple. Not recommended.
172										Tree characters desirable. Fruit attractive, large, good.
173										Not recommended.
174										Wood very brittle. Productive. Fruit small.
175										Of no value.
176										Small and poor in quality.

Abbreviations.— *Size.*— l, large; m, medium; s, small; v, very. *Form.*— a, angular; c, conical; l, light; r, red; ru, russet; s, striped; w, white; y, yellow. *Flavor.*— a, acid; b, brisk; m, mild; s, sweet; *Starring.*— *, recommended; **, well recommended; +, worthy of trial.

No.	VARIETY.	Origin.	Bearing age.	Form.	Size.	Color of skin.	Color of flesh.	Flavor.	Quality.	Use.	Season.
177	Doux	Fr.?		r o	l	y r s	w	m sa	f	k	Dec., Jan.
178	Draper	Aust'lia		o c	m	g y s r	g y	sa	f	k	Jan., Mar.
179	Du Bois	N. Y.		o	m	y r s	y	m sa	g	k	Feb., June
180	Dudley	Me.		r c	m—l	y r s	y	b sa	vg	k	Sept., Oct.
181	Dumelow	Eng.		r o	m—l	y r s	w	b sa	g	k	Nov., Mar.
182	Duncan	Eng.?		r	s—m	y r s	y	m sa	g—vg	d	Jan., May
183	Dutch Mignonne	Eu.		r o	m	y r s	y	b sa	g	d k	Jan., Apr.
184	Duzenbury	N. Y.		r ob c	m	g y r s	w y	sa	vg	d k	Feb. May
185	Dyer	Unk.		r o	m—l	g y b	w	m sa	vg—b	d	Sept., Oct.
186	Early Harvest	Am.	4 yrs.	r o	m	y	v w	sa	g—vg	d	July, Aug.
187	Early Joe	N. Y.		o c	s—m	g y r s	w	m sa	vg—b	d	Aug., Sept.
188	Early Pennock	Unk.		r	l	y r s	w	sa	f—g	k	Aug.
189	Early Ripe	Unk.		r o	m	y g	w	sa	f—g	k	Aug.
190	Early Strawberry	N. Y.		r c	m	y r s	w y	sa	vg	d	Aug.
191	Edwards Favorite	N.C.?		o	m	y g r s	w	b sa	g	k	Feb., May
192	Egg Top	Unk.		ob c	m	y r s	w	sa	f—g	d	Nov., Dec.
193	Eicke	Neb.		r c	s—m	y r s c	y	m sa	g	k	Dec., Feb.
194	Eiser	Ger.		r c	m	y r s	y w	m sa	g	k	Jan., June
195	Elgin Pippin	Ala.		r o c	l—m	y	w y	sa	g	k	Sept., Dec.
196	Ellsworth	N. Y.		r	m	y b	w	b sa	vg—b	d	Jan., Mar.
197	English Pippin	Rus.		r o c	l	g y	w y	sa	f—g	k	Sept., Nov.
198	English Russet	Unk.		r c	m	g y ru	y w	m sa	g	d	Jan., May
199	Ensee	Unk.		r o c	l	g y r s	y	m sa	g	k	Dec., Jan.
200	Eper	Unk.		r c	s	g y r s	y w	sa	m	k	Feb., May
201	Esopus *Spitzenburg*	N. Y.	9 yrs.	r c	m—l	y r s	y	sa	vg—b	d k	Nov., Feb.
202	Evening Party	Pa.		r o	m	g y r s	y	m sa	vg—b	d	Dec., Jan.
203	Ewalt	Pa.		r c	l	y r s	w	b sa	g	k	Nov., Apr.
204	Falix	Unk.		o c	m	g y r s	w y	m sa	g	k	Nov., Apr.
205	Fallawater	Pa.	5 yrs.	r	l—vl	g y b	g w	m sa	g	k	Nov., Mar.
206	Fall Greening	N. Y.		r o	m	g y	g w	sa	g—vg	d	Dec., Feb.
207	Fall Harvey	Mass.		r	l	y	w	sa	vg	d	Oct., Dec.
208	Fall Jenneting	Conn.?		r o c	l—m	g y	w	sa	g	d k	Sept., Dec.
209	Fall Orange	Unk.		r c	l—m	g y b	w	sa	vg	d k	Sept., Nov.
210	Fall Pippin	Am.	9 yrs.	r o	l—vl	g y	w	sa	vg	d k	Sept., Jan.
211	Fall Wine	Unk.		r o	m	y r s	y	m sa	vg	d	Sept., Jan.
212	Fameuse	Unk.	5 yrs.	r o	m	y r s	w	sa	vg	d	Oct., Dec.
213	Family	Ga.		r ov	s—m	y r s	y w	b sa	g	d k	Oct., Jan.
214	Fanny	Pa.		r o c	m	y r s	w y	m sa	g—vg	d	Sept., Nov.
215	Farris	Ky.		r o	m	y r s	w	sa	g	k	Dec., Mar.
216	Ferdinand	S. C.		r c	m—l	y g b	y	sa	g—vg	d	Dec., May
217	Fishkill	N. Y.		r o	l—vl	y r	w y	m sa	f—g	k	Nov., Feb.
218	Flanders Pippin	Eng.		o	l	g y b r	w	sa	g	k	Nov., Feb.
219	Florence	Ark.		r ov	m	y w r s	y	sa	g—vg	d k	Dec., May
220	Flory	O.		r c	m	y	y	sa	g	k	Oct., Feb.
221	Flushing *Spitzenburg*	Am.		r c	m—l	y g r	w	m sa	g	k	Oct., Feb.
222	Ford	N. Y.		r c	l	y	y w	b sa	g	k	Oct., Jan.
223	Forest	N. Y.		r ob c	m	y r s	y	m sa	vg	d	Dec., Mar.
224	Fraker	Kan.		r c	m	y r s	y	m sa	g	d	Dec., Apr.
225	Franchot	N. Y.		r c	m	y r s	y	sa	g	k	Oct., Jan.
226	French Paradise	Fr.		o	m	y r	w y	m s	g	k	Aug.
227	French Pippin	Unk.		r o	l—vl	y b	y	sa	g—vg	k	Jan., May
228	Frosakers	Swed.		r o	l	y b	y w	m sa	g	k	Sept.
229	Fullerton *Sweet*	N. Y.		r c	m	y	w	s	vg	d	Oct., Nov.
230	Gano	Unk.		r c	m	y r s	y w	m sa	g	k	Dec., Apr.
231	Garden Royal	Mass.		r o	m	g y r s	y	m sa	vg	d	Aug., Sept.
232	Gardner Pearmain	N. Y.		o	m	y r s	w	s	g	d	Sept.
233	Gem	Unk.		r o c	m—l	g y r s	y	m sa	f	k	Sept.
234	Genesee Flower	N. Y.		r o	l	y g	w g	m sa	g	k	Sept., Nov.
235	Gideon	Minn.	4 yrs.	r c	l—m	y	y	sa	f—g	k	Oct.

i, irregular; o, oblate; ob, oblong; ov, ovate; r, roundish. *Color.*— b, blush; c, carmine; d, dark; g, green; sa, subacid. *Quality.*— b, best; g, good; f, fair; p, poor; v, very. *Use.*— d, dessert; k, kitchen.

No.	Long Island.	Hudson Valley.	St. Lawrence and Champlain Vl'ys.	Mohawk Valley.	Eastern Plateau.	Central Lakes.	Ontario Shore.	Erie Shore.	Western Plateau.	REMARKS.
177										Not recommended.
178										Surpassed by other varieties.
179										Of Blue Pearmain type. Doubtful value.
180										Recommended where a hardy apple is wanted.
181										A standard English culinary apple, of doubtful value here.
182										Too small.
183										Tree vigorous, very productive. Fruit too small.
184										Little known outside of Putnam county where it originated.
185										One of the finest dessert apples.
186	*	*				*	*	*	*	Valuable only as an early dessert apple.
187	*	*				*	*	*	*	Of value for the home orchard only. High quality.
188										Discarded.
189										Surpassed by others of its season.
190										Planted only as a home sort.
191										Not well adapted for growing as far north as this State.
192										Nearly obsolete.
193										Not recommended.
194										Hardly worth growing.
195										Does not equal other varieties of its season.
196										Not grown outside of Columbia county.
197										Inferior to standard varieties.
198										Planted only in eastern New York.
199										Surpassed by others of its season.
200										Of no value.
201	**	**		**	**	**	**	*	*	Lacks vigor. Unproductive. Best quality. Adapted to some localities.
202										Fruit small but of high quality. Suitable for home only.
203										Tree uncertain bearer. Fruit characteristics desirable.
204										Not recommended.
205										Vigorous and productive. Fruit inferior in quality.
206										Two of this name. Neither worthy of consideration.
207										Resembles Fall Pippin; is less desirable. Very hardy.
208										Of fair quality, but easily bruised and of poor color.
209										Thrifty, hardy, good cropper. Fruit tender and poor in color.
210	**	**	*	*	**	**	**	**	**	A standard variety. Recommended.
211										Although of excellent quality, not valuable commercially.
212			**	*	*				*	Hardy, productive. Fruit scabs badly, tender, small.
213										Not desirable.
214	*	*			*	*	*	*	*	Vigorous, productive. Fruit bright red, good, small.
215										Too unattractive in color and size to be desirable.
216										May be worth planting in southeastern New York.
217				*	*	*				Worth planting in certain localities.
218										May be worthy of testing.
219										May prove valuable where Ben Davis does well.
220										Only moderately productive. Not recommended.
221										A shy bearer. Fruit drops badly. Second rate quality.
222										No longer propagated.
223										A chance seedling of doubtful value.
224										Surpassed by standard varieties.
225										Undesirable.
226										Used as a stock.
227										Not being planted in New York.
228										Without value.
229										Of no value.
230	**	**				**	**	**		Valuable where Ben Davis thrives.
231										Good dessert sort but too small for market.
232										No longer propagated.
233										Of no value.
234										Confined to western New York. Of local value only.
235										Of little value.

ABBREVIATIONS.— *Size.*— l, large; m, medium; s, small; v, very. *Form.*— a, angular; c, conical; l, light; r, red; ru, russet; s, striped; w, white; y, yellow. *Flavor.*— a, acid; b, brisk; m, mild; s, sweet; *Starring.*— *, recommended; **, well recommended; +, worthy of trial.

No.	VARIETY.	Origin.	Bearing age.	Form.	Size.	Color of skin.	Color of flesh.	Flavor.	Quality.	Use.	Season.
236	Gideon Sweet	Minn.		r c	m—l	y g r s	y	s	g—vg	d k	Nov., Apr.
237	Gilpin	Va.		r ov	m	g y b	y	m sa	g	k	Feb., June
238	Gimmersta	Swed.		r ov	s	g y r s c	y g	sa	p	k	Nov., Dec.
239	Ginnie	Ill.		o c	m—l	y r s	w	sa	g—vg	d	Sept., Nov.
240	Givens	Ark.		o r c	m	y g r s	y w	m sa	g	k	Jan., May
241	Gladstone	Eng.		r o c	m—l	g y r	y	m sa	f	k	Sept., Oct.
242	Glenloch	Tenn.		r o	l	y r s	y	m sa	g	k	Dec., Feb.
243	Gloria Mundi	Am.		r c	l—vl	g y	g y	m sa	f—g	k	Oct., Jan.
244	Golden Medal	Pa.?		r o	m	y g b	y	s	f—g	k	Dec., May
245	Golden Pearmain	N. Z.		r c	m—s	y b	y w	sa	f	k	Sept., Oct.
246	(I) Golden Pippin	Eng.		r	s	y ru	y	b sa	g—vg	d	Jan., June
247	(II) Golden Pippin	Unk.		r o	l—vl	g y	y	m sa	g—vg	d k	Sept., Dec.
248	(III) Golden Pippin	Mass.		r o	l	g y b	y	sa	g	k	Sept., Oct.
249	Golden Red	N. Y.		r o	m—s	y r s	y	m sa	g	d	Dec., Jan.
250	Golden Reinette	Eu.	13 yrs.	r o	s	g y r s	y	b sa	g	d	Oct., Jan.
251	Golden Reinette (Rus.)	Rus.		o c	m	g y		m sa	g	k	Sept., Dec.
252	Golden Russet	Eng.?	9 yrs.	r o c	m	g y ru	g y	sa	vg	d k	Dec., Apr.
253	Golden Sweet	Conn.?	9 yrs.	r o	m—l	y g	y	s	g—vg	d	Aug., Sept.
254	Golden White	Rus.		o c	m	g y r	w	s	f—g	k	Sept., Oct.
255	Golding	Am.		r o c	m	y	y	sa	g—vg	d k	Oct.
256	Good Peasant	Rus.		r o	m—l	g y r s c	y w	m sa	g	k	Sept., Oct.
257	Gracie	Minn.?		r o	l	y	y	m sa	g	d	Sept., Oct.
258	Graf Luxburg	Rus.		r o	l	g y r s c	y w	b sa	g	k	Sept., Oct.
259	Grand Duke Michel Pearmain.	Rus.		r o c	m—l	g y d r c	y g	sa	f	k	Nov., Dec.
260	Grandmother	Rus.		r ov c	m—l	g y b	w	sa	f—g	k	Nov., Jan.
261	Granite	N. H.		r ob	l	y r s	w	m sa	g—vg	d	Nov., Feb.
262	Gravenstein	Eu.	8 yrs.	o	l	y r s	y	sa	vg—b	d k	Sept., Nov.
263	Great Barbe	Rus.		o	l	y r	g w	m sa	f—g	k	Dec., Jan.
264	Great Mogul	Rus.		r ov	l	g y r s	w y	sa	f—g	k	Oct., Dec.
265	Green and Yellow Newtown.	N. Y.	5 yrs.	r o	m—vl	g y	g w	sa	b	d k	Feb., May
266	Green Seek-no-Further	N. Y.?		r c	l	y b	y	sa	vg	d	Oct., Jan.
267	Green Sweet	Am.		r ov	m	y g	g w	s	g	k	Dec., May
268	Greenville	O.		r	l—m	y b	y	m sa	g	k	Nov., Feb.
269	Greyhouse	Am.		o	m	g r	y	sa	f—g	k	Feb., May
270	Grimes	W. Va.		r ob	m—l	y	y	sa	vg—b	d k	Nov., Feb.
271	Grosh	Ohio?		r o	l—vl	g y r s	y w	sa	g—vg	k	Sept., Jan.
272	Grundy	Ia.		r ob	l	y r	w y	sa	vg	k	Sept., Oct.
273	Haas	Mo.	2 yrs.	o	m	y r s	w	b sa	f	k	Oct., Dec.
274	Hagloe	Am.?		r c	m—l	g y r s	w y	b sa	g	k	Aug., Sept.
275	Halt	Ark.	8 yrs.	r o c	l	g y r s c	w y	s	f	k	Nov., Jan.
276	Hanlon	O.	13 yrs.	o c	l	y r s	y w	s	f	k	Sept., Oct.
277	Hargrove	N. C.		r c	s—m	y v	w	m sa	g	k	Nov., Mar.
278	Hartford Rose	Conn.		ob c	m—l	y r c	w	m sa	g	k	Sept., Oct.
279	Harvest Redstreak	Pa.		o	m	y r s	w	b sa	g	k	Aug., Sept.
280	Haskell	Mass.		r o	l—m	g y b	y	s	vg	d	Sept., Dec.
281	Hawley	N. Y.		r	l—vl	g y	y	m sa	vg	d	Sept., Nov.
282	Hawthornden	Scot.		r	m—l	w y b	w	m sa	g	k	Sept.
283	Haywood	N. C.		o	m	y r s c	w y	m sa	f	k	Dec., Jan.
284	Hazen	Vt.		r	m	y g	y	s	f—g	k	Dec., Apr.
285	Headlight	Unk.		r o c	m	g y r s c	y w	m sa	f	k	Nov., Jan.
286	Hedrick	W. Va.		o c	s	g y r	g y	sa	g	k	Nov., Jan.
287	Henniker	Eng.		r o	m—l	y r s	y	sa	g—vg	k d	Nov., Mar.
288	Henry Clay Summer	Unk.		r c	m	y d r c	w	b sa	g	k	Sept., Oct.
289	Herefordshire	Eng.		r o	m	g y r	y	sa	f—g	k	Oct., Jan.
290	Herkimer	N. Y.		r ob c	m—l	g y r s c	y	b sa	g	k	Dec., Mar.
291	Hibernal	Rus.		o	l	g y r s	y	b sa	g	k	Nov., Dec.
292	Hicks	N. Y.		r	m	y r s	w	s	vg	d	Aug.
293	Hiester	Pa.		r o	m	y r s	w	m sa	f—g	k	Dec., Feb.

i, irregular; o, oblate; ob, oblong; ov, ovate; r, roundish. *Color.*— b, blush; c, carmine; d, dark; g, green; sa, subacid. *Quality.*— b, best; g, good; f, fair; p, poor; v, very. *Use.*— d, dessert; k, kitchen.

No.	Long Island.	Hudson Valley.	St. Lawrence and Champlain Vl'ys.	Mohawk Valley.	Eastern Plateau.	Central Lakes.	Ontario Shore.	Erie Shore.	Western Plateau.	REMARKS.
236										Of no value.
237										An old very late keeping variety too small to be valuable.
238										A worthless variety.
239										Unworthy.
240										Of no value.
241										Not recommended.
242										Of no value.
243										Cultivated for exhibition purposes only.
244										May be worth trial as a late keeping sweet apple.
245										Of no value.
246										Valuable as a dessert fruit in England; little known in New York.
247										Hardly as good as Fall Pippin.
248										No longer grown in New York.
249										A Long Island variety now apparently obsolete.
250										Highly esteemed in England, but little known here.
251										May be of value in the north.
252	*	*		*	*	*	*	*	*	Hardy, vigorous, productive. Small, late, excellent.
253										Suitable only for home use.
254										Not desirable.
255										Seldom or never planted in New York.
256										Not desirable.
257										Of doubtful value.
258										Of questionable value.
259										Of no value.
260										Of little or no value.
261										A New England variety of little value in New York.
262	*	**	**	*	*	*	*	*	*	Bears early, productive, vigorous. Attractive, excellent.
263										As tested here not worthy.
264										Not recommended.
265	**	**			**	*	*			Standard in quality. Succeeds in certain localities only.
266										Now seldom found in New York.
267										An old variety grown only for local markets.
268										Suitable for general market but does not excel in quality.
269										An old variety, not now generally cultivated.
270	*	*			*	*	*	*	*	Beautiful and of high quality. Not always reliable.
271										Good, but hardly equal to Gravenstein.
272										Of very doubtful value.
273										Supplanted by better kinds.
274										Not worth planting.
275										Of no value.
276										Surpassed by better varieties of its season.
277										Not worthy of trial.
278										Supplanted by better kinds
279										Not attractive in any particular.
280										Desirable for the home orchard.
281	*	*			*	*	*	*	*	Handsome and delicious, but poor tree characters.
282										Little known. Not worthy of introduction.
283										Not desirable.
284										Not recommended.
285										Of no value.
286										Not desirable.
287										Not recommended.
288										Of doubtful value.
289										Does not appear to be worthy of trial in New York.
290	+	+	+	+	+	+	+	+	+	Apparently of value.
291										Very hardy, productive, fine for cooking.
292										Not recommended.
293										Not recommended.

ABBREVIATIONS.— *Size.*— l, large; m, medium; s, small; v, very. *Form.*— a, angular; c, conical; l, light; r, red; ru, russet; s, striped; w, white; y, yellow. *Flavor.*— a, acid; b, brisk; m, mild; s, sweet; *Starring.*— *, recommended; **, well recommended; +, worthy of trial.

No.	VARIETY.	Origin.	Bearing age.	Form.	Size.	Color of skin.	Color of flesh.	Flavor.	Quality.	Use.	Season.
294	Highland	N. Y.		o	s	y b	w	m sa	vg	d	Jan., Mar.
295	Hightop Sweet	Mass.		r o	m—s	y	y	s	vg	d	July, Aug.
296	Hilaire	Can.		r o	m	y r s	w	sa	g—vg	d	Nov., Jan.
297	Hilton	N. Y.		r	l	y g		sa	g	k	Sept., Oct.
298	Hoadley	Wis.		r o	l	g y r s	y	b sa	g	k	Sept., Nov.
299	Hog Island *Sweet*	N. Y.		r c	m—l	g y r s	y	s	g—vg	d	Sept., Nov.
300	Holland Pippin	Am.		r	l—vl	g y b	w y	b sa	g	k	Sept., Oct.
301	Holland Winter	Eng.?		r c	m—l	g w b	w	sa	g	k	Dec., May
302	Holmes Sweet	N. Y.		r c	m	y b	y	s	vg	d	Nov., Feb.
303	Hook	N. Y.?		r ob c	m	g y	w y	m sa	vg	d	Oct., Nov.
304	Houghton *Sweet*	Vt.		r o	l	y b	y w	s	g—vg	d	Sept., Oct.
305	Howard Best	Ia.?		o c	l	y g r s	y	sa	f—g	k	Sept., Oct.
306	Hubbardston	Mass.	9 yrs.	r c	l	y r s	y	m sa	vg—b	d k	Oct., Jan.
307	Hunterdon	Unk.		r o c	l	y d r s c	y	sa	p	k	Dec., Jan.
308	Hunter Pippin	N. Y.		r c	m	w y	w	b sa	g	k	Aug.
309	Hunt Russet	Mass.		o	m	y r ru	y w	sa	vg—b	d	Jan., Apr.
310	Huntsman	Mo.		r o	l	y g b	y	sa	g—vg	d k	Dec., Apr.
311	Hurlbut	Conn.		r o c	m	g y r s	w y	m sa	g—vg	d	Oct., Dec.
312	Hurne	Ark. ?	8 yrs.	r o c	m—s	g y r s	g w	m sa	p	k	Jan., Mar.
313	Hyde King	Unk.		r	l—vl	y g b	w y	m sa	g	k	Dec., May
314	Ingram	Mo.		r o	m	g y r s	y w	m sa	g—vg	d k	Feb., June
315	Iowa Beauty	Ia.		r o	m	g y r s	w y	sa	g	k	Sept.
316	Isham	Wis.		r c	m	y g r s		s	g—vg	d	Oct., Dec.
317	Ivanhoe	Va.		r o	m	g y b		m sa	g—vg	d	Dec., Mar.
318	Jack	N. Y.?		o c	m—l	g y	y	m sa	g—vg	d	Oct., Nov.
319	Jackson	Pa.		r o	m	g y r s	y	m sa	g	d	Oct., Feb.
320	Jacobs Sweet	Mass.		r o c	l	y g b	w	s	g	d	Oct., Mar.
321	Jarvis	N. Y.		r o c	l	y r s	y	sa	g	k	Sept., Nov.
322	Jefferis	Pa.	4 yrs.	r o	s—m	g y r s	w y	m sa	vg	d	Sept., Jan.
323	Jefferson County	N. Y.		r o c	m	y r	y	sa	g—vg	d	Oct., Nov.
324	Jenkins Seedling	Unk.		r c	m	y b	w g	a	p	k	Dec., Mar.
325	Jersey Black	Unk.		r o	m—l	y d r s	y w	m sa	g	d	Nov., Feb.
326	Jersey Sweet	Unk.		r c	m	y r s	w y	s	g—vg	d	Sept., Dec.
327	Jewett Red	N. H.		r o	m	y r s		m sa	g—vg	d	Oct., Feb.
328	Johnson	Wis.		r o	l	g y r	y	sa	f	k	Dec., Feb.
329	Johnsonite	Unk.		r c	l	g r s	y	sa	f	k	Jan., Apr.
330	Jonathan	N. Y.		r c	m	y r s	y	sa	vg—b	d k	Nov., Jan.
331	Jonathan Buler	Ill.?		o	l—m	y g r s	w	m sa	f—g	k	Nov., Apr.
332	Jones Seedling	Unk.		r o	m	g y b	g w	sa	g	k	Jan., Mar.
333	Judson	Ia.	9 yrs.	r c	vl—l	y r s	w y	b sa	f—g	k	Oct., Nov.
334	July	Rus.		r c	m	w y r s	y	sa	f—g	k	July, Sept.
335	Kaighn	N. J.		ob c	l	y r s	y	sa	g	k	Nov., Jan.
336	Kalkidon	Rus.		o c	l—m	g y r s	y	m sa	f—g	k	Sept., Jan.
337	Kansas Greening	Kan.		r c	m	g b	y	m sa	f—g	k	Jan., Apr.
338	Kansas Keeper	Kan.?		r c	m—l	y g r s	y	sa	f—g	k	Dec., June
339	Karabovka	Rus.	9 yrs.	o	s—m	g y r s	w	m sa	f—g	k	Aug., Sept.
340	Kecskemet	Eu.		o	l	g y r	y w	sa	f	k	Nov., Dec.
341	Kentish Fillbasket	Eng.		r o	vl	g y b	w	b sa	g	k	Oct., Dec.
342	Keswick	Eng.	3 yrs.	r c	m—l	g y b	y w	b sa	g	k	Aug., Sept.
343	King David	Ark.		r o c	l	y d r	y	b sa	g	k	Nov., Jan.
344	King of Pippins	Eng.		r o	s—m	y r s	y	b sa	g	k	Nov., Dec.
345	Kinnaird	Tenn.	6 yrs.	o c	m—l	y r	y	sa	g—vg	d k	Dec., Mar.
346	Kirkbridge	Am.		ob c	s—m	y w	w	sa	g—vg	d	Aug., Sept.
347	Kirkland	N. Y.		r c	l—m	y b	y	sa	g	k	Jan., May
348	Kittageskee	N. C.?		r o c	s—m	y b	y	m sa	vg	d	Dec., May
349	Lacker	Pa.		r o	m—l	y g r s	w	m sa	g—vg	d	Dec., May
350	Lady	Fr.	12 yrs.	o	s—vs	y b	w	sa	g—vg	d	Dec., May
351	Lady Finger	Unk.		r c	m	y r	g w	sa	g—vg	d	Aug.
352	Lady Sweet	N. Y.	9 yrs.	r c	l—m	y g r s	w y	s	vg—b	d k	Nov., Apr.
353	Landon	Vt.		r o c	m—l	y r s c	y	m sa	g—vg	d	Dec., May

i, irregular; o, oblate; ob, oblong; ov, ovate; r, roundish. *Color.*— b, blush; c, carmine; d, dark; g, green; sa, subacid. *Quality.*— b, best; g, good; f, fair; p, poor; v, very. *Use.*— d, dessert; k, kitchen.

No.	Long Island.	Hudson Valley.	St. Lawrence and Champlain Vlys.	Mohawk Valley.	Eastern Plateau.	Central Lakes.	Ontario Shore.	Erie Shore.	Western Plateau.	REMARKS.
294										Lady type. Suitable for localities where Lady thrives.
295										Should be dropped from cultivation.
296										Worthy of trial in Fameuse regions.
297										Passing out of cultivation.
298										May be grown where the Oldenburg thrives.
299										Little known and unworthy.
300										Resembles Fall Pippin, but poorer in quality.
301										Greening type. Keeps well.
302										A Niagara county seedling now practically obsolete.
303		*	*	*	*					Unattractive, but excellent.
304										Desirable for the local fall market.
305										Resembles Alexander.
306	**	**		*	*	**	**	*	*	Bears early, productive. Fruit handsome and good.
307										A worthless variety.
308										Of no commercial value.
309										Superseded by more valuable russet kinds
310										Quality excellent but of doubtful value.
311										Not being planted.
312										Of no value.
313										Surpassed by Rhode Island Greening.
314										A seedling of and similar to Ralls.
315										Not desirable.
316										Not desirable.
317										Not recommended.
318										Neither tree nor fruit characters are desirable.
319										Not recommended.
320										Planted only in home orchards.
321										Not recommended.
322	*	*			*	*	*	*	*	Excellent for the home orchard.
323										Not worth planting.
324										Worthless for commercial purposes.
325										Attractive in color but valueless.
326	*	*			*	*	*	*	*	One of the best sweet apples for home use.
327			*	*						One of the best in quality of the Blue Pearmain type.
328										Surpassed by better kinds of its season.
329										Not desirable.
330	**	**		*	**	*	*	*	*	Excellent but small in New York.
331										Fruit attractive in size and color. Lacks quality.
332										Not recommended.
333										Not worthy.
334										Inferior to Tetofsky which it resembles.
335										Obsolete.
336										Very inferior.
337										Not worthy.
338										A late keeper. Succeeds better in Southern latitudes.
339										Unworthy.
340										Of no value.
341										Many worthier sorts of its season.
342										Suitable for home use only.
343	+	+	+	+	+	+	+	+	+	Appears promising as a commercial sort.
344										Surpassed by other kinds.
345										Winesap type. Not adapted to New York.
346										Not recommended.
347										Tree characters good. Fruit of good color and keeps well.
348										A late keeping dessert apple for home use.
349										Gradually passing out of cultivation.
350	*	*		*	*	*	*	*	*	A beautiful fancy apple suitable for special trade.
351										Several varieties under this name. Of no value.
352	*	**		*	*	*		*	*	One of the most desirable of the sweet apples.
353										Shy bearer. Good color and size.

ABBREVIATIONS.— *Size.*— l, large; m, medium; s, small; v, very. *Form.*— a, angular; c, conical; l, light; r, red; ru, russet; s, striped; w, white; y, yellow. *Flavor.*— a, acid; b, brisk; m, mild; s, sweet; *Starring.*— *, recommended; **, well recommended; +, worthy of trial.

No.	VARIETY.	Origin.	Bearing age.	Form.	Size.	Color of skin.	Color of flesh.	Flavor.	Quality.	Use.	Season.
354	Landsberg	Ger		r o	m—l	g y b	y	m sa	g—vg	d	Oct., Jan.
355	Lankford	Md		r o	m	g y r s	y	m sa	f—g	k	Dec., May
356	Lansingburg	O		r o	m	y g r s c	g y	m sa	f—g	k	Dec., May
357	Late Strawberry	N. Y		r ob c	m	y r s	y w		vg	d	Sept., Dec.
358	Latham	N. Y		o c	m	y r	w	m sa	g	d	Nov., Dec.
359	La Victoire	Can		o c	l—m	g y r s	w	m sa	g	d	Nov., Dec.
360	Lawver	Kan.?		r o	m	d r	w y	b sa	f—g	k	Jan., May
361	Lead	Rus		o c	m	g y r s	w	sa	f	k	Aug., Sept.
362	Lee Sweet	N. Y.?		r ob c	m—l	y r s	w y	s	g	k	Jan., Apr.
363	Legal Tender	Ark.?	8 yrs.	r o	l	g d r	g w	sa	g	k	Feb., May
364	Lehigh *Greening*	Pa		r o c	m—l	y g	y	m sa	g	k	Jan., May
365	Lilly *of Kent*	Del		r o c	l	y g	g y	sa	g	d	Jan., May
366	Limbertwig (small or red).	Unk		r o c	m	y r s	y	sa	g	k	Jan., Apr.
367	Limbertwig (large or green).	Larger, greener and less attractive in color than the above, coarser, more juicy and much inferior in flavor and quality.									
368	Lincoln Pippin	Conn		r o c	m	g y	w y	sa	vg	d	Oct., Dec.
369	Lindenwald	N. Y		r o	m	y b	y	sa	g—vg	d	Sept.
370	Lombard	Vt		r o	m—l	g y b	y w	sa	g	k	Nov., Dec.
371	Longevity	Can		r c	l	g y r	y	sa	g	k	Jan., Mar.
372	Longfield	Rus	4 yrs.	r o c	m	y b	w	sa	g	d	Sept., Oct.
373	Long Island Pearmain	Unk		ob	l	y r s	....	sa	g	d	Oct., Jan.
374	(I) Long Island Russet	N. Y		ob c	s	y ru	y	m sa	g	d	Oct., Feb.
375	(II) Long Island Russet	Unk		r ob c	m—s	y ru	y	b sa	vg	d	Nov., Jan.
376	Long Keeper	Va		r c	m—s	g r s	g w	b sa	f—g	k	Jan., Apr.
377	Long Red Pearmain	Unk		o c	m—l	y r s	....	sa	g	k	Nov., Dec.
378	Long Stem	Several varieties under this name, all worthless.									
379	Long Stem of Penn	Pa		r o	m	y g r s	w	b sa	g—vg	d	Nov., Feb.
380	Longworth	Ia		r o c	m	w y r s	w	m sa	vg	d	Nov., Feb.
381	Lord Seedling	N. Y		r ob c	m	y	y w	m sa	g—vg	d k	Sept., Oct.
382	Lord Suffield	Eng		r c	l	y	w	sa	g	k	July, Sept.
383	Lou	Minn		r ob c	m—l	y r s	y w	sa	f—g	k	Aug.
384	Louise	Can		r c	m	g y b	w	sa	vg	d	Oct., Feb.
385	Lowell	Am		r ob c	l	y	y	sa	g—vg	d k	Aug., Oct.
386	Lowland Raspberry	Rus		r c	m—l	w r s	w	m sa	vg	d	Aug.
387	Lubsk Queen	Rus		r		w r	w	sa	g	k	Aug., Sept.
388	Luckey	N. Y		r c	m—s	g y d r c	y g	sa	f	k	Nov., Feb.
389	Lyscom	Mass		r	l—v l	y g r s	w y	sa	g	k	Oct., Dec.
390	Mabie	N. Y		r ob	l—m	y r s	y	s	g	k	Nov., Dec.
391	McAfee	Ky		r o	m—l	y r s	y w	m sa	g—vg	k	Oct., Feb.
392	McCarty	A strain of Pumpkin Sweet. Smaller and keeps longer.									
393	McCroskey	Tenn		r c	m	y d r	y	sa	f	k	Dec., Feb.
394	MacDonough	N. Y		r o	m	y	....	m sa	f—g	k	Aug., Sept.
395	McIntosh	Can	6 yrs.	r	m—l	y r s	w	m sa	vg—b	d	Oct., Dec.
396	McKinley	Ind	9 yrs.	r o	m—l	y r s	y	sa	g	d	Dec., Jan.
397	McKinney	N. Y		o	m—l	y b	w y	m sa	g	k	Jan., Apr.
398	McLellan	Conn		r o c	l—m	g y r s	w	m sa	vg	d	Oct., Feb.
399	McMahon	Wis	4 yrs.	r c	l—v l	g y w	w	b sa	f—g	k	Oct., Jan.
400	Magenta	Unk		o c	l—m	y g b	y	sa	g—vg	k	Nov., Mar.
401	Magog	Vt		r ob	m—l	g y r s	y	sa	g	k	Oct., Jan.
402	Magyar	Unk		r c	l	y b	w y	sa	f	k	Dec., Mar.
403	Maiden Blush	N. J	4 yrs.	o	m	y b	w	sa	g	k	Sept., Nov.
404	Maiden Favorite	N. Y		r c	m	w y	w	sa	g—vg	d	Oct., Jan.
405	Mala Carle	Italy		o c	m	y b	w	sa	g	d	Dec., Feb.
406	Malinda	Vt		r c	l—m	y b	w	m sa	f	k	Jan., Apr.
407	Mammoth	Ark	8 yrs.	r o	l	g y	y w	s a	f	k	Dec., Mar.
408	Manchester	Unk		r ob c	m—l	g y r s	w	b sa	g—vg	d	Dec., Apr.
409	Mann	N. Y		r o	m—l	g y	y	sa	f—g	k	Jan., Apr.
410	Manwaring	Kan		r c	m	y b	y	b sa	g	k	Oct., Jan.

i, irregular; o, oblate; ob, oblong; ov, ovate; r, roundish.   *Color.*— b, blush; c, carmine; d, dark; g, green; sa, subacid.   *Quality.*— b, best; g, good; f, fair; p, poor; v, very.   *Use.*— d, dessert; k, kitchen.

No.	Long Island.	Hudson Valley.	St. Lawrence and Champlain Vl'ys.	Mohawk Valley.	Eastern Plateau.	Central Lakes.	Ontario Shore.	Erie Shore.	Western Plateau.	REMARKS.
354	...	...	...	...	...	...	...	...	...	Excelled by standard sorts.
355	...	...	...	...	...	...	...	...	...	Easily excelled by standard varieties.
356	...	...	...	...	...	...	...	...	...	Very late keeper but poor in quality.
357	...	...	...	...	...	...	...	...	...	One of the good dessert apples of its season.
358	...	...	...	...	...	...	...	...	...	Obsolete.
359	...	...	...	...	...	...	...	...	...	A seedling of Fameuse inferior to McIntosh.
360	...	...	...	...	...	...	...	...	...	Better adapted to southern latitudes.
361	...	...	...	...	...	...	...	...	...	Unworthy.
362	...	...	...	...	...	...	...	...	...	Grown about Geneva where it is held in high esteem
363	...	...	...	...	...	...	...	...	...	Surpassed by other kinds.
364	...	...	...	...	...	...	...	...	...	Surpassed by other sorts of its class.
365	...	...	...	...	...	...	...	...	...	Not sufficiently tested in New York.
366	...	...	...	...	...	...	...	...	...	A southern variety not adapted to New York.
367										
368	...	...	...	...	.	...	...	...	...	Grown only about Syracuse.
369	...	...	...	...	...	...	...	...	...	Known only in Columbia County.
370	...	...	...	...	...	...	...	...	...	Not recommended.
371	+	+	+	+	+	+	+	+	+	Not fully tested. Attractive and appears promising.
372	...	...	...	...	...	...	...	...	...	Grown for home use and local markets.
373	...	...	...	...	...	...	...	...	...	Obsolete.
374	...	...	...	...	...	...	...	...	...	Now nearly obsolete.
375	...	...	...	...	...	...	...	...	...	Represented now only by old trees.
376	...	...	...	...	...	...	...	...	...	Not recommended.
377	...	...	...	...	...	...	...	...	...	Obsolete.
378										
379	...	...	...	...	...	...	...	...	...	Not recommended.
380	...	...	...	...	...	...	...	...	...	Unworthy.
381	+	+	+	+	+	+	+	+	+	New and recommended for home orchards.
382	...	...	...	...	...	...	...	...	...	So susceptible to blight as to be worthless.
383	...	...	...	...	...	...	...	...	...	Excelled by its parent, Oldenburg.
384	...	...	...	...	...	...	...	...	...	A beautiful and excellent apple for home use.
385	*	*	...	.	*	*	*	*	*	Desirable for home use and local market.
386	+	+	+	+	+	+	+	+	+	A beautiful dessert fruit.
387	...	...	...	...	...	...	...	...	...	Not recommended.
388	...	...	...	...	...	...	...	...	...	Surpassed by other kinds.
389	...	...	...	...	...	...	...	...	...	Supplanted by best sorts.
390	...	...	...	...	...	...	...	...	...	Surpassed by Victoria Sweet which it resembles.
391	...	...	...	...	...	...	...	...	...	A seedling of Lawver, not adapted to New York.
392										
393	...	...	...	...	...	...	...	...	...	Not recommended.
394	...	...	...	...	...	...	...	...	...	Not likely to become popular.
395	*	**	**	**	**	**	**	**	**	One of the best sorts of its season.
396	...	...	...	...	...	...	...	...	...	Not recommended.
397	...	...	...	...	...	...	...	...	...	An Ulster county seedling—not known elsewhere.
398	...	...	...	...	...	...	...	...	...	Choicely good. Adapted to fancy market.
399	...	...	...	...	...	...	...	...	...	Less desirable than standard kinds of its season.
400	...	...	...	...	...	...	...	...	...	Appears to be identical with Canada Reinette.
401	...	...	...	...	...	...	...	...	...	Not valuable enough to retain.
402	...	...	...	...	...	...	...	...	...	Not desirable.
403	*	*	...	*	*	*	*	*	*	Worthy of planting for home or market, where it succeeds.
404	...	...	...	...	...	...	...	...	...	No longer propagated.
405	...	...	...	...	...	...	...	...	...	Does not succeed as far north as New York.
406	...	...	...	...	...	...	...	...	...	Desirable only when hardiness is a prime requisite.
407	...	...	...	...	...	...	...	...	...	Not recommended.
408	...	...	...	...	...	...	...	...	...	Of Esopus *Spitzenburg* type but inferior to that variety.
409	...	...	...	...	...	...	...	...	...	A hardy, productive tree. Long keeper of fair quality.
410	...	...	...	...	...	...	...	...	...	Not recommended.

ABBREVIATIONS.— *Size.*— l, large; m, medium; s, small; v, very. *Form.*— a, angular; c, conical; l, light; r, red; ru, russet; s, striped; w, white; y, yellow. *Flavor.*— a, acid; b, brisk; m, mild; s, sweet; *Starring.*— *, recommended; **, well recommended; +, worthy of trial.

No.	VARIETY.	Origin.	Bearing age.	Form.	Size.	Color of skin.	Color of flesh.	Flavor.	Quality.	Use.	Season.
411	Margaret	Eng.		r c	s—m	y r s	w	s a	g	d	July, Aug.
412	Marigold	Eng.?		r c	m—l	y g b	y	m s a	g	d	Nov., Apr.
413	Mason Orange	Kan.		ob c	m—l	y b	y	s a	g	d k	Nov., Feb.
414	Masten	N. Y.		r c	m	g y b	w	s a	g	k	Dec., Feb.
415	Mellott	Pa.?		r c	m	g y r s	y	m s a	g	k	Dec., Feb.
416	Melon	N. Y.	4 yrs.	r o c	l—m	y g r s	w	s a	vg	d	Oct., Jan.
417	Ménagère	Eu.		o c	l—vl	y b	w	s a	f	k	Oct., Jan.
418	Merrill	N. Y.		r	m	y b	y	s a	g	d	Dec., Mar.
419	Mexico	Conn.?		r o	l	g y d r	y w	b s a	g—vg	k d	Sept., Oct.
420	Middle	N. Y.		r ob c	m	g y	w	b s a	vg	d	Dec., Mar.
421	Mihalyfi	Eu.		r	m—s	y b	y	m s a	g	k	Jan., Mar.
422	Milam	Unk.		r c	s—m	y g r s	y	m s a	g	d	Nov., Jan.
423	Milden	N. H.		o c	l—m	y r s	w y	s a	g	d k	Nov., Jan.
424	Miller	N. Y.		r o c	l	y r s	y	s a	g—vg	d	Oct., Nov.
425	Milligen	Pa.		r o c	l	y r s	y	s a	g—vg	d	Oct., Jan.
426	Milwaukee	Wis.		o	l—m	y r s	y	b s a	f—g	k	Oct., Jan.
427	Minister	Mass.		r ob c	l—m	y g r s	y w	b s a	g—vg	d k	Nov., Feb.
428	Minkler	Pa.?		r o c	m	y g r s	y	m s a	f—g	k	Nov., Apr.
429	Missing Link	Unk.		r	l	g y r	y	m s a	f	k	Jan., Apr.
430	Missouri *Pippin*	Mo.		r c	m	g y r s	w	b s a	f—g	k	Oct., Jan.
431	Mock	Ark.		r o c	m—l	g y d r	y	s a	f	k	Jan., Mar.
432	Mon Desire	Rus.		r o	l	y b	w y	b s a	g	k	Nov., Dec.
433	Monmouth	N. J.	5 yrs.	r o c	l—m	y b	y	b s a	g—vg	d k	Nov., Jan.
434	Monroe *Sweet*	Unk.		r o c	m	y r c	y	s	g	d	Sept., Oct.
435	Montgomery	N. Y.		r o c	l	g w r s	w	b s a	g	k	Sept., Oct.
436	Moon	Ga.		r o	m	y g b	w	m s a	g	k	Nov., Apr.
437	Moore Extra	Ohio		r o c	l	g y r s	y	s a	f	k	Nov., Jan.
438	Moore Sweet	Mass.		r o c	m—l	y g r	y	s	g	k	Nov., Apr.
439	Morgan Seedling	Am.		o	m	g y r	y w	m s a	f	k	Dec., Jan.
440	Mosher	N. Y.		o c	m	g y	y	s	g	d	Sept., Oct.
441	Mother	Mass.	9 yrs.	r c	m	y r s	y	m s a	vg—b	d	Sept., Jan.
442	Mountain Sweet	Pa.		r o c	m	y r s	w	s	g	d	Sept., Dec.
443	Mouse	N. Y.		r c	l	g y b	w	m s a	g	k	Oct., Nov.
444	Moyer	Ind.?		ob c	l	y b	w	m s a	g—vg	d	Dec., Apr.
445	Munroe Favorite	Aust'lia.		r o c	m	y	w y	a	f	k	Nov., Jan.
446	Munson	Mass.?	5 yrs.	r o	m	g y b	y	s	g—vg	d	Sept., Dec.
447	Nassau	N. Y.		o	m	y r s	y w	s a	g	k	Dec., Mar.
448	Nelson	Ill.		r ob ov	m	g y b	g y	s	g	d k	Feb., May
449	Nero	N. J.	6 yrs.	r c	m	g y r s	w	m s a	g—vg	k	Jan., Apr.
450	Newark Pippin	N. J.?		r ob	m—l	g y	y	s a	vg—b	d k	Nov., Feb.
451	Newman	O.		ob c	m—l	y g b	y	m s a	f—g	k	Dec., May
452	Newtown Spitzenburg	N. Y.		r o	m	y r s	y	m s a	vg—b	d	Nov., Feb.
453	New Water	Pa.?		o c	l—m	g y r s	w y	m s a	g	d	Oct., Feb.
454	Nickajack	N. C.		r c	l—m	g y r s	y	m s a	g	k	Dec., May
455	Nitchner Strawberry	Rus.		r c	l	y r s c	w	s a	g	k	Sept.
456	Northern Spy	N. Y.	13 yrs.	r c	l—vl	y r s	y w	s a	vg—b	d k	Dec., Feb.
457	Northern Sweet	Vt.		r o	m	y b	w	s	vg	d	Sept., Oct.
458	Northwestern Greening	Wis.		r c	m—l	y g	y	m s a	g	d k	Dec., Mar.
459	Norton Red	Unk.		r o c	m	y d r	y	m s a	g	d	Nov., Mar.
460	Nyari Piros	Unk.		r o c	l	g y r	g w	m s a	f	k	Sept.
461	Oak	N. Y.?		r c	m—l	y	w y	s a	g	k	Sept., Oct.
462	Oakland	Mich.		r o c	m—l	g y r s	w	s	g	d k	Nov., Feb.
463	Occident	Cal.		r o c	m	y b	w y	s a	vg	d k	Jan., May
464	Oel Austin	N. Y.		r c	m	y r s	y w	m s a	f—g	d k	Nov., Mar.
465	Ogdensburg	N. Y.		r o c	m	y b	w	m s a	vg	d	Nov., Dec.
466	Ohio Nonpareil	O.		r o	m—l	y r s	y w	s a	g—vg	d	Oct., Nov.
467	Ohio Pippin	O.		r o c	m	y b	y	m s a	g	d	Sept., Jan.
468	Okabena	Minn.		o	l	y r s	y	s a	vg	d	Dec.
469	Oldenburg	Rus.	2 yrs.	r o	m—l	g y r s	y w	s a	g—vg	k	Aug., Sept.
470	Old Garden	Vt.		r c	s—m	y b	y	s	f—g	k	Sept., Oct.

i, irregular; *o*, oblate; *ob*, oblong; *ov*, ovate; *r*, roundish.   *Color.*— *b*, blush; *c*, carmine; *d*, dark; *g*, green; *sa*, subacid.   *Quality.*— *b*, best; *g*, good; *f*, fair; *p*, poor; *v*, very.   *Use.*— *d*, dessert; *k*, kitchen.

No.	Long Island.	Hudson Valley.	St. Lawrence and Champlain Vl'ys.	Mohawk Valley.	Eastern Plateau.	Central Lakes.	Ontario Shore.	Erie Shore.	Western Plateau.	REMARKS.
411										Without value.
412										Does not excel standard varieties of its season.
413										Almost identical with Yellow Bellflower.
414										A Dutchess county apple unknown elsewhere.
415										Of no value.
416	*	*		*	*	*	*	*	*	Choicely good for the home orchard.
417										Suitable only for exhibition purposes.
418										Unknown outside of Chenango county.
419										Not fully tested. Appears to have value.
420										Less valuable than other varieties of its season.
421										Of no value.
422										Valuable in the south only.
423										Succeeds only in northern and elevated regions.
424										Unknown outside of Orange county.
425										Attractive but excelled by standard sorts.
426										Succeeds in the northern part of the State.
427										It has failed to win favorable recognition in New York.
428										Not a promising variety.
429										A long keeper but does not rank high in quality. Southern.
430										Does not develop marketable size in New York.
431										Of no value.
432										Not fully tested in New York.
433										Good cropper, uncertain keeper, variable in size.
434										Possibly of value for the home orchard only.
435	+	+	+	+	+	+	+	+	+	Promising but not fully tested.
436										Unsatisfactory in this region.
437										Of no value.
438										A good keeper, good cropper, moderately attractive.
439										Of no value.
440										Without special value.
441	*	*			*	*	*	*	*	Tree characteristics poor. Appearance and quality of the best.
442										Of little value.
443										Nearly obsolete.
444										Similar to Yellow Bellflower. Surpassed by other sorts.
445										Not desirable.
446										Has given place to better sorts.
447	+	+	+	+	+	+	+	+	+	Of superior quality.
448										A late keeping sweet apple. Unattractive.
449										Not valuable.
450										An old variety now nearly obsolete in this State.
451										Of Yellow Bellflower group. Not recommended.
452										Not a good commercial sort. Excellent in quality.
453										Not superior to standard sorts of its season.
454										Not adapted to northern regions.
455										Not worth planting.
456	*	**	*	**	**	**	**	**	**	Tardy bearer. Vigorous. Highest quality. A standard.
457										Hardiness alone commends it.
458										Similar to Rhode Island Greening; hardier, not so good.
459										Appears to be of value, though not sufficiently tested.
460										Of no value.
461										Surpassed by other varieties.
462										Popular in Michigan. Unknown in New York.
463										Similar to Yellow Bellflower.
464										Blue Pearmain group. Adapted to cold climate.
465										Not now grown.
466										Tree characters poor; of doubtful value.
467										Possibly worthy of attention.
468										Nothing to recommend it.
469	**	**	**	**	**	**	**	**	**	Hardy, vigorous, productive, cosmopolitan.
470										Of no value.

ABBREVIATIONS.— *Size.*— l, large; m, medium; s, small; v, very. *Form.*— a, angular; c, conical; l, light; r, red; ru, russet; s, striped; w, white; y, yellow. *Flavor.*— a, acid; b, brisk; m, mild; s, sweet; *Starring.*— *, recommended; **, well recommended; +, worthy of trial.

No.	VARIETY.	Origin.	Bearing age.	Form.	Size.	Color of skin.	Color of flesh.	Flavor.	Quality.	Use.	Season.
471	Olga	Rus.		r o	l	g y r s	g w	s	g	k	Aug.
472	Olive	N. C.		r c	s	y r s	y	m sa	f—g	k	Nov., Feb.
473	Oliver	Ark.		r o	l—m	g y r s	y w	sa	g	k	Dec., Mar.
474	Olympia	See description of Baldwin.									
475	Onondaga	N. Y.	6 yrs.	r c	l	g y d r s	w y	sa	g	k	Nov., Jan.
476	Ontario	Can.		r o c	l	g y r s	w y	b sa	g—vg	d k	Nov., Mar.
477	Opalescent	O.?		r c	l—vl	y d r	y w	m sa	g—vg	d	Oct., Jan.
478	Orange	Several varieties under this name, all worthless in New York.									
479	Orange Pippin	At least two varieties of this name. Neither of value in New York.									
480	Orange Sweet	Several varieties under this name. Worthless in New York.									
481	Oranie	Swed.		r o	l	g y	y w	m sa	f	k	Aug.
482	Ornament	Eu.		r o c	m	y r s	w	m sa	g	d	Oct., Feb.
483	Ortley	N. J.		ob c	l—m	w y b	w	sa	vg	d k	Oct., Feb.
484	Ostrakoff	Rus.		r	m	y	w	b sa	f—g	k	Nov., Dec.
485	Oswego	N. Y.	6 yrs.	r c	l	g y d r s	y	b sa	vg	d	Dec., Apr.
486	Oszi Vaj	Unk.		r c	m	g w r	w g	m sa	f	k	Aug.
487	Otsego	N. Y.	4 yrs.	r ob c	m	y d r s c	y	m sa	g	d	Nov., Feb.
488	Overton	Ark.?		b c	l	g y r	y w	m sa	f	k	Nov., Feb.
489	Ozone	Ark.	8 yrs.	o c	s	y d r	y	m sa	f	k	Dec., Jan.
490	Palmer	N. Z.		r o	m—l	g y	g y	b sa	g	k	Dec., Feb.
491	Palouse	Wash.		ob c	l	y r s	y	sa	vg	d	Oct., Dec.
492	Paragon	Tenn.		r c	m—l	g y r s	y	sa	g—vg	d k	Jan., May
493	Park	N. Y.		r c	m—l	y r s	y	m sa	vg	d	Dec., Mar.
494	Parlin	Me.		r o c	m—l	y r s	y	m sa	g	d	Oct., Feb.
495	Parry White	Pa.?		r ov	m	y w b	w	sa	g	d	Aug., Sept.
496	Parson	Mass.		r c	l	y r	w	s	g—vg	d	Nov., Feb.
497	Patten	Ia.		r o	m—l	g y b	y	sa	g	k	Oct., Jan.
498	Paul Long	Rus.		r c	m	g y r	y w	s	g	k	Oct., Nov.
499	Pawpaw	Mich.		r ob c	l	y r s	y	sa	g—vg	d	Dec., June
500	Payne	Mo.		r c	m	g y r s	y	m sa	g—vg	d	Jan., June
501	Peach	Unk.		o c	m	y b	w	b sa	g—vg	d	Dec., May
502	Peach (Montreal)	Fr.		r ob c	l	y w b		sa	g	d k	Sept.
503	Peach Blow	Me.		r o c	l	g y b	y	sa	f	k	Oct., Nov.
504	Peach Pond	N. Y.		o c	m—s	y r s		s	vg	d	Sept., Nov.
505	Pear	Pa.		r ob	s	y r s	y w	m sa	f	k	Sept., Nov.
506	Pearsall	N. Y.		r	l	y r s	y	s	g	k	Nov., Jan.
507	Pease	Conn.		r c	l—m	y g r s c	w y	sa	g—vg	d	Oct., Jan.
508	Peasgood	Eng.		r o	l	y r s	y	sa	g	k	Sept., Oct.
509	Peck *Pleasant*	R. I.	7 yrs.	r o c	m—l	y b	y	sa	vg—b	d k	Nov., Feb.
510	Pennock	Pa.		r o c	l	g y r s	y	m sa	f—g	k	Dec., Apr.
511	Peron	Mex.		r ob c	s	y b	g w	b sa	p	k	Jan., Mar.
512	Perry	O.		o	m	y r s	y	sa	g	k	Jan., May
513	Perry Red	N. Y.		o	m	y r s	w	sa	g—vg	d	Oct.
514	Perry Russet	R. I.?		r o c	m—l	y ru	y	sa	g	d k	Dec., Feb.
515	Persian	Rus.	10 yrs.	r ob	s	y r	w	m sa	g	k	Sept.
516	Peter	Minn.		r o	m	y r s	y	m sa	g—vg	d k	Sept., Oct.
517	Pewaukee	Wis.	5 yrs.	r o	m—l	y g r s	w	sa	f—g	k	Nov., Apr.
518	Pickard	Ind.		r o	l	g y b	y	sa	vg	d	Nov., Feb.
519	Pifer	Pa.		r o	m	g v r s	y	m sa	f	k	Jan., July
520	Pine Stump	N. C.		r o	m	y r	y	sa	g	k	Nov., Feb.
521	Pioneer	Aust'lia.		r c	m	y b	g w	sa	f—g	k	Jan., Apr.
522	Plumb Cider	O.?		r c	m	y r s	w	b sa	g	k	Oct., Jan.
523	Pomme Grise	Fr.?	5 yrs.	o r	s	y ru	y	sa	vg—b	d	Dec., Feb.
524	Pomona	Eng.		o c	m—vl	g y r s	w	sa	g—vg	k	Sept., Oct.
525	Porter	Mass.		ob c	s—l	y b	y	sa	g—vg	d k	Sept., Nov.
526	Pound Sweet	This name has been applied to several varieties of large sweet apples.									
527	Pratt *Sweet*	N. Y.		r c	l	y r s	y w	s	vg	d	Dec., Mar.
528	Priestly	Pa.		r ob	l—m	g y r s	y	m sa	g	d k	Dec., Apr.
529	Primate	N. Y.	3 yrs.	r o c	m—l	y g b	w	sa	vg—b	d	Aug., Sept.
530	Prince Albert	Eu.		r c	l	y g r s	y	b sa	g	k	Nov., Feb.

i, irregular; o, oblate; ob, oblong; ov, ovate; r, roundish. *Color.*— b, blush; c, carmine; d, dark; g, green; sa, subacid. *Quality.*— b, best; g, good; f, fair; p, poor; v, very. *Use.*— d, dessert; k, kitchen.

No.	Long Island.	Hudson Valley.	St. Lawrence and Champlain Vl'ys.	Mohawk Valley.	Eastern Plateau.	Central Lakes.	Ontario Shore.	Erie Shore.	Western Plateau.	REMARKS.
471										Not desirable.
472										Unworthy of consideration.
473										Too small to be valuable.
474										The same as Baldwin.
475	+	+	+	+	+	+	+	+	+	Resembles McIntosh.
476										Similar to Northern Spy; hardier. Inferior in quality.
477	+	+	+	+	+	+	+	+	+	Worth planting commercially.
478										
479										
480										
481										Not recommended.
482										Surpassed by other dessert apples of its season.
483										Yellow Bellflower group. Of good quality but skin tender.
484										Of no value.
485	+	+	+	+	+	+	+	+	+	Very similar to Northern Spy. Very promising.
486										Of no value.
487	+	+	+	+	+	+	+	+	+	Probably of value for fancy market.
488										Not recommended.
489										Not desirable.
490										Not recommended.
491										An inferior seedling of Tompkins King.
492										A southern variety not adapted to New York.
493										Probably obsolete.
494										Of no value.
495										Resembles Early Harvest. Later.
496										Of no value.
497										Seedling of Oldenburg. Worth trying in the North.
498										Of no value.
499										Not recommended.
500										Probably not well suited to this State.
501										Not recommended.
502										Cannot displace Oldenburg which is of the same season.
503										Not recommended.
504										Long known, but has failed to establish itself.
505										A worthless variety.
506										A Queens County seedling; apparently obsolete.
507										Grown for home use and local market.
508										Scarcely tested; of no value.
509										Shy bearer, subject to diseases. Fruit excellent.
510										Not desirable.
511										Type of Lady. Worthless.
512										Surpassed by better varieties.
513										Not valuable.
514										Excelled by other russets of its season.
515										Of no value.
516										Resembles Wealthy and does not surpass it.
517										Desirable only when hardiness is a prime requisite.
518										Not valuable.
519										Not recommended.
520										Not adapted to New York conditions. Southern.
521										Of no value.
522										Should give place to better sorts.
523										A small russet of high quality. Not profitable commercially.
524										An English sort of little value in America.
525	*	*		*	*	*	*		*	Has many merits for home use and local market.
526										
527										An old variety now practically obsolete.
528										Surpassed by standard varieties.
529	*	*	*	*	*	*	*	*	*	Tree characters poor. Valuable for dessert and local market.
530										Of no value.

ABBREVIATIONS.— *Size.*— l, large; m, medium; s, small; v, very. *Form.*— a, angular; c, conical; l, light; r, red; ru, russet; s, striped; w, white; y, yellow. *Flavor.*— a, acid; b, brisk; m, mild; s, sweet; *Starring.*— *, recommended; **, well recommended; +, worthy of trial.

No.	VARIETY	Origin.	Bearing age.	Form.	Size.	Color of skin.	Color of flesh.	Flavor.	Quality.	Use.	Season.
531	Prince Double	Rus.		r c	l	g y r s	y w	sa	f	k	Sept., Oct.
532	Princess Fossia	Rus.		r c	m	g y ru	y	m sa	g	k	Nov., Feb.
533	Princess Wilhelma	Rus.		o c	m	y b	w	a	f—g	k	Nov., Dec.
534	Prolific Sweeting	Rus.		r o	m	w y	w	s	g	d	Sept., Oct.
535	Pryor	Va.?		r o	m—l	g y r s	y	sa	vg—b	d k	Dec., Mar.
536	Pumpkin Russet	N. Eng.	9 yrs.	r o	l	g y ru	wy	s	g	k	Sept., Oct.
537	Pumpkin Sweet	Conn.	9 yrs.	r c	l—vl	g y	w	s	g	k	Oct., Jan.
538	Purity	Unk		r o c	l	g y b	g w	sa	f	k	Sept., Oct.
539	Queen	Unk		o	l	g y r s	g w	b sa	g	k	Oct., Dec.
540	Queen (West)	Unk		o	m	y b	g y	sa	g	k	Jan., Mar.
541	(I) Quince (of Cole)	Me.		r o c	l—vl	y b	y w	b sa	g—vg	k	July, Sept.
542	(II) Quince (of Coxe)	N. Y.?		r o	l	y	y w	sa	g—vg	k	Nov.
543	Ralls	Va.?	5 yrs.	r o c	m	y r s c	w y	sa	vg	d k	Dec., May
544	Rambo	Pa.?		r o	m	g y r s	g w	m sa	g—vg	k	Nov., Dec.
545	Ramsdell Sweet	Conn.?		ob c	l—m	y r s	y	vs	g—vg	d k	Oct., Feb.
546	Raspberry	Rus.		ob	s	y r		sa	vg	d	July, Aug.
547	Red and Green *Sweet*	Unk		ob c	l—vl	y r s	w	s	f—g	k	Aug., Sept.
548	Red Astrachan	Rus.	5 yrs.	r c	m—l	y r s	w	b sa	g—vg	d k	Aug., Sept.
549	Red Canada	N. Eng.?		r c	m	y r s	w	m sa	g—b	d k	Nov., Mar.
550	Red Carver	Pa.		r o c	m—l	g y r s	y w	m sa	f	k	Oct., Dec.
551	Red Hook	N. Y.		r c	l—vl	y r s		sa	g	k	Aug., Sept.
552	Red June	N. C.		r o	s—m	y r	w	b sa	g—vg	d k	Aug., Oct.
553	Red Queen	Rus.?		r c	l	g y b	g y	sa	p	k	Nov., Jan.
554	Red Russet	A bud sport of Baldwin differing only n having a russet skin. Considered less valuable than Baldwin.									
555	Redstreak	Eng.		ob	s	y r s	y	sa	g	k	Dec., Apr.
556	Red Transparent	Rus.		r	m	y r	g w	sa	g—vg	k	Aug.
557	Red Wine	Eu.		r o	m	w r	v w	sa	g	k	Aug., Sept.
558	Red Winter Sweet	Ill.		r o c	m	y b	y w	s	g	k	Dec., Feb.
559	Reed	N. Y.		r	m	y w r s	w	sa	g	k	Nov.
560	Regmalard	Fr.?	12 yrs.	r o	l	g y b	y	sa	g	k	Nov., Jan.
561	Reinette Pippin	Fr.		o	m—l	w y	w	sa	g	d k	Oct., Feb.
562	Rensselaer	N. Y.	5 yrs.	r c	l	y b r	y	sa	g	d	Dec., Feb.
563	Repka	Rus.	9 yrs.	r o c	m—s	y w	w	m sa	g	k	Aug., Sept.
564	Repka Malenka	Rus.		r c	m—s	y r s		m sa	g	k	Jan., Apr.
565	Rhode Island *Greening*	R. I.	5 yrs.	r o	l	y g	y	sa	vg	d k	Oct., Mar.
566	Ribston	Eng.		r c	m—l	y r s	y	sa	vg	d k	Oct., Dec.
567	Richard Early Winter	Unk		r ob c	l	y r s	w y	m sa	f	k	Oct., Dec.
568	Richard Graft	N. Y.		r o	m	y r s	y	sa	vg	d	Sept.
569	Ridge	Pa.?		r ob c	l—m	y b	w y	m sa	g	k	Feb., May
570	Ringstads	Swed.		r o c	m—s	g r s	g w	sa	g	k	Aug., Sept.
571	Rioter	Unk		r o	m—s	g y r s	y w	m sa	f	k	Sept., Oct.
572	Rittenhouse	N. J.		r o c	m	y b	y	s	g	k	Oct., Nov.
573	Rock Pippin	Ohio?		r o	m	y g b	w y	sa	g	k	Feb., June
574	Rockland	N. Y.		r o	m—l	y d r s c	y	sa	g	d k	Nov., Jan.
575	Rolfe	Me.		r o	m—l	y b	w y	b sa	g	k	Oct., Dec.
576	Roman Stem	N. J		r	m—s	w y b	y	sa	vg	d	Oct., Dec.
577	Romanite	Unk		r c	s	y r	y	sa	g	d k	Mar., July
578	Rome	O.	2 yrs.	r o c	l	g y r s	y	sa	g	k	Nov., Mar.
579	Romna	Rus.		o c	m—l	g y r	w y	b sa	f—g	k	Sept., Jan.
580	Ronk	Ind.		r o	m	y r	w	sa	g	d	Oct., Feb.
581	Roseau	Eu.?		o	m—l	g r		sa	g	k	Dec., Feb.
582	Rose Red	N. Y.?		o	m	w r s	w	sa	vg	d	Sept., Nov.
583	Roxbury	Mass.		r o	l—m	y ru	y	g—vg	d k	Dec., May
584	Ruby Gem	N. Y.?		o	m	g y r s	g w	m sa	g	k	Sept.
585	Rudolph	Eu.		r o	m	g y r	w y	b sa	g	k	Nov., Feb.
586	Russian Baldwin	Rus.		r o	m	y r s	y w	m sa	g	k	Jan., May
587	Rutherford	Ark.	13 yrs.	r ob c	m	g y r s c	y	sa	p	k	Jan., Apr.
588	Rutledge	Tex.		r	m	y r s	y	m sa	f—g	k	Nov., May
589	Safstaholms	Swed.		ob c	m—l	y r s	w	m sa	g	d	Oct., Dec.

i, irregular; o, oblate; ob, oblong; ov, ovate; r, roundish. *Color.—* b, blush; c, carmine; d, dark; g, green; sa, subacid. *Quality.—* b, best; g, good; f, fair; p, poor; v, very. *Use.—* d, dessert; k, kitchen.

No.	Long Island.	Hudson Valley.	St. Lawrence and Champlain Vl'ys.	Mohawk Valley.	Eastern Plateau.	Central Lakes.	Ontario Shore.	Erie Shore.	Western Plateau.	REMARKS.
531										Not valuable.
532										Of no value.
533										A worthless variety.
534										May be grown in northern New York.
535										Not well adapted to this region. Southern.
536										Should give place to others of better quality.
537	**	**		*	*	**	**	**	*	Valued for home and market purposes.
538										Of no value.
539										May be identical with Buckingham. Of no value.
540										Not recommended.
541										Supplanted by better sorts.
542										Obsolete.
543										Too small. Blossoms very late.
544										Tender tree; productive to a fault; excellent quality.
545										Without commercial value.
546										A substitute for Red June where that sort winter kills.
547										Of no value.
548	**	**	**	**	**	**	**	**	**	Succeeds under many conditions. Home and local markets.
549	*	*	*	*	*	**	**	*	*	Excellent.
550										Not recommended.
551										Grown only in the vicinity of Red Hook, N. Y.
552										Small, scabby, imperfect in New York.
553										A worthless variety.
554										
555										An old cider variety now obsolete in New York.
556										Without value where Primate can be grown.
557										Worthless.
558										Not recommended.
559										Not worth planting.
560										Well thought of in France but of little value in New York.
561										Excelled by Rhode Island Greening.
562	+	+	+	+	+	+	+	+	+	Type of Jonathan with high flavor.
563										Much inferior to Primate with which it competes.
564										Fruit too small to be valuable.
565	**	**	*	**	**	**	**	**	**	The standard green apple of New York.
566										Belongs with Hubbardston which greatly excels it.
567										Of no value.
568										Of but little value outside of the Hudson Valley.
569										Excelled by others of its season.
570										Cannot be recommended.
571										Not recommended.
572										Of no value.
573										One of the latest keepers.
574	+	+	+	+	+	+	+	+	+	Of excellent quality.
575										Tree very hardy, otherwise without merit.
576										Superseded by better sorts.
577										Not recommended.
578	**	**		*	*	**	**	**	*	A standard commercial variety.
579										Not worthy of attention.
580										Worthless.
581										Identity not certain.
582										Discarded.
583	**	**	*	**	**	**	**	**	**	A leading commercial variety.
584										Not valuable.
585										Of no value.
586										May be valuable in northern New York.
587										Of no value.
588										Of doubtful value. Very hardy.
589										Of very doubtful value.

ABBREVIATIONS.— *Size.*— l, large; m, medium; s, small; v, very. *Form.*— a, angular; c, conical; l, light; r, red; ru, russet; s, striped; w, white; y, yellow. *Flavor.*— a, acid; b, brisk; m, mild; s, sweet; *Starring.*— *, recommended; **, well recommended; +, worthy of trial.

No.	VARIETY.	Origin.	Bearing age.	Form.	Size.	Color of skin.	Color of flesh.	Flavor.	Quality.	Use.	Season.
590	Sailee Russet	N. Y.		o c	m	g ru	w	sa	g	d	Dec.
591	Sailly	N. Y.		r c	m	g y b	....	sa	g	k	Sept.
592	St. Lawrence	Am.		o c	l—m	y r s c	w	m sa	g—vg	d	Sept., Oct.
593	St. Peter	Rus.		r o	s	g y r s	w	m sa	f	k	Aug.
594	Salisbury	N. Y.		r	m—l	y	....	sa	g—vg	d k	?
595	Salome	Ill.		r o c	m	y r s	w y	sa	g—vg	d k	Nov., Mar.
596	Sandy Glass	Rus.		r o	l—m	g y b	w	b sa	f—g	k	Sept., Nov.
597	Saratoga	N. Y.	5 yrs.	r o c	l	g y r	w y	sa	g	k	Jan., Apr.
598	Savewell	N. Y.		r o c	m	w y b	y	sa	g	k	Feb., Mar.
599	Saxton	Mass.?		r o	m	y r s	y	sa	g—vg	d	Sept.
600	Scarlet Cranberry	Va.		r o	m	y r s	w	m sa	f—g	d	Feb., May
601	Scarlet Pippin	Can.		r	m	y r s	w	m sa	vg	d k	Oct., Dec.
602	Schenectady	N. Y.	5 yrs.	r c	l	g y r c	y w	sa	g	k	Nov., Jan.
603	Schodack	N. Y.?		r o	m	y g r	w y	b sa	f—g	k	Feb., June
604	Schoharie	N. Y.	6 yrs.	r ob c	l	y d r s	y	m sa	g	k	Nov., Mar.
605	Schoonmaker	Unk.		r o	l	g y b	y w	b sa	vg	d k	Jan., Mar.
606	Schuyler *Sweet*	N. Y.		r o	l	y	w	s	g—vg	d	Sept., Oct.
607	Scollop Gilliflower	Eu.?		r c	m—l	y r s	y	m sa	g	k	Nov., Feb.
608	Scott	Vt.		r o c	m	g y r s	y w	b sa	g	k	Dec., Mar.
609	Scott Best	N. Y.		r o	m—l	y r s	w	sa	g—vg	d	Nov., Dec.
610	Scribner	N. Y.		r c	m	y r s	w y	sa	vg	d	Dec., Feb.
611	Sekula	Unk.		o	l	g y d r	g w	m sa	f	k	Dec., Mar.
612	Seneca	N. Y.		r ob c	l	y b	y	sa	vg	d	Nov., Jan.
613	Shackleford	Mo.		r ov	m—l	g y r s	y	m sa	f—g	k	Nov., Apr.
614	(I) Shannon	Ark.		o c	l	w y b	y	sa	g—vg	d k	Nov., Apr.
615	(II) Shannon	O.		r o c	l—m	y b	w y	m sa	g	d k	Nov., Apr.
616	Sharp	Md.?		r o	m	w	w	m sa	vg	d	Sept., Oct.
617	Sheddan	Tenn.		r o	l—m	g y r b	y	m sa	g—vg	d	Jan., May
618	Shepherd Perfection	Unk.		r o c	m	g y d r	y	m sa	g	d	Nov., Jan.
619	Sheriff	Pa.		r o	m—s	y r s	w	m sa	g	k	Dec., Feb.
620	Sherman	N. Y.		o	m	g y b	....	s	g—vg	d	Nov., Jan.
621	Shiawassee	Mich.		o c	m—l	y r s	v w	sa	g—vg	d	Oct., Jan.
622	Shirley	Texas		r o c	m—s	y r s	w	m sa	f—g	k	Dec., May
623	Sigfried	Unk.		o c	m	g r s	g w	b sa	g	k	Mar., May
624	Sine-Qua-Non	N. Y.		r c	m	g y	w	m sa	g	d	Aug.
625	Skank	Unk.		r c	l	y r s	y	m sa	g—vg	d	Oct., Feb.
626	Skelton	Ark.	7 yrs.	r c	l	g y r s	y	m sa	f—g	k	Aug., Sept.
627	Sleight	A facsimile of Lady, except it is larger and ripens earlier. Not known outside of Dutchess County.									
628	Slingerland	N. Y.		r o	m—l	y r s	w	sa	g—vg	d	Dec., Feb.
629	Smith Cider	Pa.		r o c	m—l	g y r s	w	sa	g	k	Nov., Mar.
630	Smokehouse	Pa.		r o	m—l	g y r s	y	m sa	g	d k	Oct., Mar.
631	Snyder	Pa.?		r o	m	g b	w y	sa	f	k	Feb., May
632	Somerset (N. Y.)	N. Y.?		r c	m—s	w y ru	w	sa	vg—b	d	Sept., Oct.
633	Sops-of-Wine	Eng.	5 yrs.	r	m	g y r	w	m sa	g	k	Aug., Oct.
634	Sour Bough	N. Y.		r c	m	y	w	b sa	g	k	Sept.
635	Spasovka	Rus.		r o	l	g y r s	g w	sa	f	k	Aug.
636	Spectator	N. Y.		r ob	m	y b	y	sa	f—g	k	Sept.
637	Springdale	Ark.		r o	m	y r s c	g y	m sa	f	k	Jan., Mar.
638	Springport	N. Y.		r ob	m	g y	y w	sa	vg	k	Dec., May
639	Stanard	N. Y.		r o c	l	g y r s	y w	b sa	g—vg	k	Oct., Mar.
640	Stark	O.		r c	l—m	y r s	y	m sa	f—g	k	Jan., June
641	Starkey	Me.		o c	m—l	y r s	w	sa	vg	d	Oct., Jan.
642	Starr	N. J.	6 yrs.	r o	vl—l	y g	w	sa	vg	d	Aug., Sept.
643	Stayman Winesap	Kan.		r c	m—l	y r s	y	sa	g—vg	d	Dec., May
644	Sterling	Mass.		r c	l	y r	y	m sa	vg	d	Dec., Apr.
645	Sterns	N. Y.		o c	l	y r	y	m sa	g	k	Sept., Nov.
646	Stewart Seedling	Unk.		r c	m	g y r	g w	sa	g	k	Jan., Apr.
647	Stillman	N. Y.		r c	s	y b	y	sa	g	k	July, Aug.
648	Stone	Vt.?		r c	l	y d r s	w y	m sa	g—vg	d k	Nov., Feb.

i, irregular; o, oblate; ob, oblong; ov, ovate; r, roundish. *Color.*— b, blush; c, carmine; d, dark; g, green;
sa, subacid. *Quality.*— b, best; g, good; f, fair; p, poor; v, very. *Use.*— d, dessert; k, kitchen.

No.	Long Island.	Hudson Valley.	St. Lawrence and Champlain Vl'ys.	Mohawk Valley.	Eastern Plateau.	Central Lakes.	Ontario Shore.	Erie Shore.	Western Plateau.	REMARKS.
590										Inferior to Roxbury.
591										Discarded.
592										Suitable only for northern regions.
593										Not valuable.
594										Known only in the vicinity of Cortland. Value doubtful.
595										Excelled by standard sorts.
596										Worthless.
597	+	+	+	+	+	+	+	+	+	Type of Ben Davis but quality much superior.
598										Worthless.
599										Worthless.
600										Southern. Does not mature here.
601										Worth planting where Fameuse succeeds.
602	+	+	+	+	+	+	+	+		Promising as a good market variety.
603										Valuable only as a remarkably late keeper.
604	+	+	+	+	+	+	+	+	+	Type of Northern Spy. Promising.
605										Worthless.
606										Probably lost to cultivation.
607										Obsolete.
608										Valuable in elevated and northern regions.
609										Has no recognized value.
610										Probably obsolete.
611		+	+	+	+	+	+	+	+	New and worth testing.
612										Possibly of value for the home orchard.
613										Ben Davis group but less desirable.
614										Resembles Ohio Pippin. Lacking in productiveness.
615										Worthless.
616										Resembles Maiden Blush but is not equal to that variety.
617										Surpassed by better varieties.
618										But little tested in New York. May have value.
619										Very hardy. Of no consequence otherwise.
620										Worthless.
621										Excelled by McIntosh, which it resembles.
622										Ben Davis group but inferior to that sort.
623										Of no value as far north as New York.
624										Supplanted by better sorts.
625										Of high quality.
626										Not recommended.
627										
628										Of no value.
629										Unsatisfactory and unprofitable in New York.
630										Its cultivation is not being extended in New York.
631										A good keeper.
632										Without merit.
633										Superseded by better varieties.
634										Unprofitable for any purpose.
635										Of no value.
636										Without value.
637										Not recommended.
638										Unproductive and unprofitable.
639										Worthless.
640	*	*		*	*	*	*		*	Considered valuable in some sections of New York.
641										Appears to be worthy of testing for the north.
642										Worthy of testing where a fruit of its type is desired.
643										Not adapted to New York.
644										Apparently obsolete.
645										Of the Alexander type. No better than that variety.
646										Of no value.
647										Discarded.
648			**							Blue Pearmain group. Valuable in Northern New York.

ABBREVIATIONS.— *Size.*— l, large; m, medium; s, small; v, very. *Form.*— a, angular; c, conical; l, light; r, red; ru, russet; s, striped; w, white; y, yellow. *Flavor.*— a, acid; b, brisk; m, mild; s, sweet; *Starring.*— *, recommended; **, well recommended; +, worthy of trial.

No.	VARIETY.	Origin.	Bearing age.	Form.	Size.	Color of skin.	Color of flesh.	Flavor.	Quality.	Use.	Season
649	Stowe	Me.		r c	m—l	g y b	y	sa	g	k	Dec., Mar.
650	Streaked Pippin	N. Y.		r ob c	l	g y r s	w y	sa	g—vg	d k	Nov., Mar.
651	Striped Gilliflower	Unk.		r ob c	l—vl	y w r s	y w	b sa	f—g	k	Sept.
652	Striped July	Tenn.		r o c	s—m	g y r s	y w	sa	g	k	Aug., Sept.
653	Striped Winter	Rus.	10 yrs.	r ov	m	g y r s	y	m sa	f	k	Sept.
654	Stroat	N. Y.		r c	m—l	y g	y	b sa	g—vg	d	Sept., Nov.
655	Strode	Pa.		ob c	m	y	y	sa	g—vg	d	Sept., Nov.
656	Stuart Golden	O.		r o	m	y b	w y	m sa	vg	d	Dec., May
657	Stump	N. Y.	7 yrs.	r ob c	m—s	w y r s	w y	sa	vg	d	Sept., Oct.
658	Stymus	N. Y.		o c	m	y r s	w	m sa	vg	d	Oct., Nov.
659	Suffolk	N. Y.		r o	m	y w	w	sa	g	k	Aug., Sept.
660	Summer Bellflower	N. Y.		r ob c	m—l	y	w	sa	g	k	Aug., Sept.
661	Summer Harvey	N. B.?		r o	l	g y b	w	b sa	g	k	Aug.
662	Summer Pearmain	Am.		r ob c	m	g y r	y	m sa	b	d	Aug., Sept.
663	Summer Queen	Unk		r c	m—l	y r s	y	sa	g—vg	k	Aug., Sept.
664	Summer Rambo	Fr.		o	l—vl	y r s	y	m sa	g	k	Sept., Nov.
665	Summer Redstreak	N. Y.		r o c	m	y r s	w	b sa	g	k	Sept.
666	Summer Rose	N. J.		r o	s—m	y r s	w	m sa	g—vg	d k	July, Aug.
667	Summer Spitzenburg	N. Y.		r c	m	w r s	y w	sa	g—vg	d	Aug., Sept.
668	Summer Sweet	Conn.		o c	m	y ru	w	s	g—vg	k	Sept.
669	Summer Wafer	Ala.?		o	m	g y d r c	y	sa	f	k	Sept., Oct.
670	Superb Sweet	Mass.		r c	m	g y r s c	g w	s	f	k	Sept., Oct.
671	Sutton	Mass.	9 yrs.	r	m	y r s	w	m sa	g—vg	d k	Nov., Mar.
672	Swaar	N. Y.		r o	l—m	g y	y	m sa	vg—b	d	Nov., Apr.
673	Swayzie	Can.		r o c	s	y ru	g y	m sa	vg—b	d	Dec., Mar.
674	Sweet and Sour	Unk.		o	m—l	y g	y	sa	f—g	k	Dec., Feb.
675	Sweet Bough	Am.		r ob c	l—m	g y	w	s	g—vg	d k	Aug., Sept.
676	Sweet Fall Pippin	N. Y.		o	l	g y	....	s	g	d k	Oct., Nov.
677	Sweet Greening	Mass.?		r o	m—l	y g b	w	s	g—vg	k	Dec., Apr.
678	Sweet Jonathan	Mo.?		r ov	m	y d r	g y	s	f	k	Nov., Feb.
679	Sweet King	N. Y.		r c	m	y r s	w	s	g—vg	d	Oct., Mar.
680	Sweet Romanite	Unk.		r o	m	g y r s	y w	s	g	k	Dec., Mar.
681	Sweet Russet	Unk.		o	m	y ru	w	s	g—vg	d	Nov., Mar.
682	Sweet Winesap	Pa.		r c	m—l	w y r s	w y	s	g—vg	d k	Nov., Apr.
683	Swenker	Pa.?		r o c	m—l	y r s	y	m sa	f	k	Nov., Mar.
684	Switzer	Rus.		r o	m	w y r	w	m sa	g	d	Aug., Oct.
685	Sylvester	N. Y.		r o	m—s	w b	v w	b sa	vg	k	Sept., Oct.
686	Tart Bough	Two varieties under this name both of which are worthless.
687	Taylor Seedling	Kan.?		r o	m—s	y b	y	s	f—g	k	Sept.
688	Terdika	Rus.		r o c	m	y g r	y w	m sa	g	k	Jan., Mar.
689	Tetofsky	Rus.	4 yrs.	r o c	m—s	g y r s	w	sa	f—g	k	July, Aug.
690	Tewksbury	N. J.		r c	s—m	y b	y	b sa	g	k	Jan., May
691	Texas	Unk.		r o c	m	y r c	y	m sa	g	k	Jan., May
692	Thaler	Almost identical with Yellow Transparent which excels it.
693	Thompson	Ia.	5 yrs.	r c	m	w y r s	w	sa	f—g	k	Oct., Dec.
694	Tinmouth	Vt.		r o	m—l	g y b	w y	m sa	g	k	Oct., Dec.
695	Tioga	N. Y.		r o c	l	w y b	y	b sa	g	k	Dec., Mar.
696	Titovka	Rus.		r ob	l	g y r s	y w	sa	g—vg	k	Aug., Sept.
697	Titus Pippin	N. Y.		ob c	l—m	g y	w y	sa	g—vg	d k	Nov., Mar.
698	Tobias	Vt.		o	m	y	y	sa	f—g	k	Nov., Apr.
699	Tobias Black	Vt.		r o	m—l	y g r s	g y	m sa	f—g	k	Nov., Apr.
700	Tobias Pippin	Vt.?		o c	m	y	w y	m sa	g	d k	Oct., Feb.
701	Tolman *Sweet*	Mass.	8 yrs.	r	m	y	w	s	g—vg	d k	Nov., Jan.
702	Tompkins King	N. J.?	5 yrs.	r c o	l—vl	y r s	y	sa	vg—b	d k	Oct., Jan.
703	Tom Putt	Eng.		r o c	l	y r s	g w	sa	f—g	k	Nov.
704	Transparent de Cronals	Rus.		r o	l	g y	y w	b sa	g	k	Sept.
705	Tufts	Mass.		r	l	y g r	y	m sa	f—g	d	Oct., Jan.
706	Twenty Ounce	Conn.	5 yrs.	r c	vl	g y r s	w y	sa	g	k	Sept., Dec.
707	Twenty Ounce Pippin	Unk.		r o	l—vl	g y r s	y	sa	f—g	k	Oct., Feb.

i, irregular; o, oblate; ob, oblong; ov, ovate; r, roundish. *Color.*— b, blush; c, carmine; d, dark; g, green; sa, subacid. *Quality.*— b, best; g, good; f, fair; p, poor; v, very. *Use.*— d, dessert; k, kitchen.

No.	Long Island.	Hudson Valley.	St. Lawrence and Champlain Vl'ys.	Mohawk Valley.	Eastern Plateau.	Central Lakes.	Ontario Shore.	Erie Shore.	Western Plateau.	REMARKS.
649										A Maine seedling worthless in New York.
650										Has many good qualities for local market.
651										Obsolete.
652										Of no value.
653										Resembles Pewaukee. Not a winter apple. Of no value.
654										Passed from cultivation.
655										Surpassed by standard sorts.
656										Not recommended.
657	*	*		*	*	*	*	*	*	Desirable for home use and for local market.
658										Worthless.
659										Lost to cultivation.
660										Dropped by the American Pomological Society.
661										Not recommended.
662										Of value only as an amateur's fruit.
663										Worthless.
664										An old sort possibly worthy of re-testing.
665										Worthless.
666										Becoming obsolete.
667										Esteemed by some for home use.
668										Discarded.
669										Of no value.
670										Not recommended.
671	*	**		*	*					Desirable only in the Hudson Valley.
672	*	*		*	*	*	*	*	*	One of the best for the amateur. Requires deep, rich loam.
673										Similar to but inferior to Pomme Grise.
674										Worthless except as a curiosity.
675	**	**		**	**	**	**	**	**	A universal favorite for the home orchard and local market.
676										Gradually going out of cultivation.
677										Esteemed for home use. Seldom planted.
678										Not recommended.
679										Not cultivated outside of Nassau County. Worthless.
680										Not recommended.
681										Several known by this name. All worthless.
682	**	**		*	*	*	*	*	*	Attractive, excellent quality; reliable cropper; overbears.
683										Does not excel standard sorts for any purpose.
684										Resembles the Fameuse but inferior.
685										Without value.
686										
687										Of no value.
688										Not recommended.
689										Surpassed by other sorts of its season.
690										Not recommended.
691										Not recommended.
692										
693										Not worth planting.
694										Not desirable.
695	+	+	+	+	+	+	+	+	+	Very promising. Resembles Northern Spy except in color.
696										Perhaps worthy of planting in the North.
697										Good tree characters. Fruit attractive and well flavored.
698										Not worthy attention except for hardiness.
699										Hardy but not equal to standard varieties.
700										Not worth planting.
701	**	**		**	**	**	**	**	**	Hardy, vigorous, early bearer, reliable cropper.
702	*	*		*	**	**	**	*	**	Were the tree hardier, healthier, longer lived and more productive, it would be more commonly grown.
703										Unworthy.
704										Worthless.
705										Resembles the Baldwin; is less desirable.
706	**	**	*	*	*	**	**	**	*	One of the best fall varieties for home or market.
707										Often confused with Twenty Ounce. Of poor quality.

ABBREVIATIONS.— *Size.*— l, large; m, medium; s, small; v, very. *Form.*— a, angular; c, conical; l, light; r, red; ru, russet; s, striped; w, white; y, yellow. *Flavor.*— a, acid; b, brisk; m, mild; s, sweet. *Starring.*— *, recommended; **, well recommended; +, worthy of trial.

No.	VARIETY	Origin	Bearing age	Form	Size	Color of skin	Color of flesh	Flavor	Quality	Use	Season
708	Tyre	N. Y.		r o	m	y r s	w	b sa	g	k	Sept.
709	Ulysses	N. Y.		o c	m	g y r s	y w	sa	f	k	Nov., Dec.
710	Upp	O.		o c	m	y r	y	sa	f	k	Dec., Feb.
711	Utter	Ill.?		r o	l—m	w y r s	w	m sa	g	k	Oct., Dec.
712	Vandevere	Del.	5 yrs.	r o	m	y r s	y	m sa	g—vg	k	Oct., Jan.
713	Vandevere Improved	Mo.?		The same as Vandevere.							
714	Vandevere Pippin	Pa.?		o c	l	y r s	w	b sa	g	k	Sept., Nov.
715	Vanhoy	N. C.		r o	m	y g r s	y	m sa	f	k	Jan., May
716	Ver	Unk.		r c	m	g y d r	w	s	f—p	k	Sept., Nov.
717	Via	Va.		r o	m	y r	y	sa	g	k	Dec., Feb.
718	Victoria Sweet	N. Y.?		r o c	m—l	y r s	y	s	g—vg	d k	Oct., Jan.
719	Victuals and Drink	N. J.		r o c	l	g y b	w y	s	p	k	Sept.
720	Vineuse Rouge	Rus.		r o c	m—l	g y r s	w	sa	g—vg	k	Aug.
721	Virginia Greening	Va.?		o	m	g y b	y	m sa	f—g	k	Feb., June
722	Voronesh Red Summer	Rus.		r o	m	y r s c	w	sa	f	k	Aug., Sept.
723	Wabash Red	Ind.?		r o	l—m	y r s	w y	m sa	g	d	Dec., May
724	Wagener	N. Y.	4 yrs.	r o	m—l	y r s	y	sa	vg—b	d k	Oct., Feb.
725	Walbridge	Ill.		r c	m	w y r s	w	m sa	f—g	k	Nov., Feb.
726	Walker Beauty	Pa.		r c	m—l	y b	y	b sa	g	k	Nov., Apr.
727	Wallace Howard	Ga.		r o b	l—m	y r s	y w	m sa	g	d	Nov., Mar.
728	Wandering Spy	Ark.		r c	l—m	y r	w	sa	g	k	Jan., Apr.
729	Washington Royal	Mass.		r o	m	g y b	w	m sa	g—vg	d	Oct., Mar.
730	Washington Strawberry	N. Y.		r c	l	g y r s c	y	sa	g—vg	d	Oct., Dec.
731	Water	Pa.		r o b c	m	g y b	w	m sa	g	d	Oct., Dec.
732	Watwood	Ky.		o	m	w y b	y w	sa	g	k	Dec., May
733	Wealthy	Minn.	6 yrs.	r o c	l—m	y r s	y w	sa	g—vg	d k	Oct., Jan.
734	Wells	Md.		r	l	w g r s	y	sa	vg	d	Nov., Mar.
735	Westchester	N. Y.	4 yrs.	r c	l	y b r	y	m sa	g—vg	d k	Nov., Jan.
736	Western Beauty	For description, see Grosh.									
737	Westfield	Conn.	9 yrs.	r c	m	y r s	y w	m sa	vg—b	d	Oct., Feb.
738	Whinery	O.		r o c	m—l	g y r b	y w	sa	f—g	k	Jan., Apr.
739	White Astrachan	Rus.		r o	m	y w	w	b sa	g	k	Aug.
740	White Doctor	Pa.		r o	l	g y	w	m sa	f—g	k	Nov., Mar.
741	White Juneating	Eng.		r o	s	y w	w	sa	g—vg	k	Aug.
742	White Pearmain	Unk.		r o b c	m	g y b	y	m sa	vg—b	d k	Dec., Mar.
743	White Pippin	Unk.		r o	m—l	g y	w	sa	g—vg	d k	Nov., May
744	White Spanish	Spain		r o	vl	y g	y w	sa	vg	d k	Oct., Jan.
745	William Prince	Unk.		o c	m—s	g w r s	w	m sa	f—g	d k	Aug.
746	Williams	Mass.	3 yrs.	r o b c	m	y d r s	y w	m sa	g	d	Aug., Sept.
747	Willis Sweet	N. Y.		r	l	y r s	w	s	vg	d k	Aug., Sept.
748	Willow	Va.?		r o c	l—m	y g r s	y g	sa	f—g	k	Jan., May
749	Willsboro	N. Y.		r c	m	y r s	y w	sa		k	Dec., Feb.
750	Windsor	Wis.	7 yrs.	r c	m	y g r	y	m sa	g—vg	d	Dec., Apr.
751	Wine	Del.		r o	m	y r s	y w	sa	g—vg	k	Oct., Mar.
752	Wine Rubets	Rus.		r	m—s	g b		m sa	f—g	k	Aug.
753	Winesap	N. J.?	5 yrs.	r c	s	y r s	y	sa	g—vg	d k	Jan., Apr.
754	Winter Banana	Ind.	5 yrs.	r o c	l	w y b	y	m sa	g—vg	d k	Nov., Jan.
755	Winter Paradise	Pa.		r o	l	g y b	w	s	vg	d	Nov., Mar.
756	Winter Pearmain	Several different varieties known under this name.									
757	Winter St. Lawrence	Eng.		r c	m—l	g y r s	w	sa	g	d	Nov., Jan.
758	Winthrop Greening	Me.		o	l	y g	w	sa	g	k	Sept.
759	Wismer	Can.	9 yrs.	r	m—l	y r s	y w	m sa	g—vg	d	Jan., Apr.
760	Wolf River	Wis.	6 yrs.	r o c	vl	g y r s	w	sa	f—g	k	Sept., Dec.
761	Workaroe	Rus.		r c	m—l	y r s	y w	m sa	g	k	Sept.
762	Yellow Bellflower	N. J.	9 yrs.	r o b c	m—vl	w y b	y	b sa	g	k	Dec., Apr.
763	Yellow Calville	Rus.		o c	m	y	w	sa	f—g	k	Aug.
764	Yellow Forest	La.	8 yrs.	r o	s—m	g y b	g w	m sa	g	d	Jan., June
765	Yellow Transparent	Rus.	4 yrs.	r o c	m	w y	w	sa	g—vg	d k	July, Aug.
766	Yopp	Ga.		r o c	m—l	g y b	w	sa	f—g	k	Oct., Nov.
767	York			Golden Pippin and Fall Pippin often pass under this name.							

i, irregular; o, oblate; ob, oblong; ov, ovate; r, roundish.   *Color.*— b, blush; c, carmine; d, dark; g, green; sa, subacid.   *Quality.*— b, best; g, good; f, fair; p, poor; v, very.   *Use.*— d, dessert; k, kitchen.

No.	Long Island.	Hudson Valley.	St. Lawrence and Champlain Vl'ys.	Mohawk Valley.	Eastern Plateau.	Central Lakes.	Ontario Shore.	Erie Shore.	Western Plateau.	REMARKS.
708										Worthless.
709										A worthless variety.
710										Of no value.
711										Without value.
712										Passing out of cultivation.
713										
714										No longer listed by nurserymen.
715										Not desirable. Southern.
716										Worthless.
717										Not recommended.
718										A good sweet apple.
719										Worthless.
720										Worthless.
721										Valued in the South as a late keeper.
722										Of no value.
723										Tree qualities good. Attractive, high quality, late keeper.
724	*	*		*	*	*	*	*	*	Early bearer; heavy cropper; short lived. Good.
725										Of little value.
726										Unproductive and not desirable.
727										Southern. Of no value.
728										Of no value.
729										Not recommended.
730										Has failed to establish itself in the commercial orchards.
731										Dropped by the American Pomological Society.
732										Inferior to standard varieties.
733	**	**	**	**	**	**	**	**	**	Tree and fruit characters good. Small on old trees.
734										Worthless.
735	+	+	+	+	+	+	+	+	+	Type of Green Newtown.
736										
737										Tree qualities good. Uncertain in adaptability.
738										Not recommended.
739										Discarded by the American Pomological Society.
740										Not recommended.
741										Has nothing to recommend it.
742										Not recommended.
743										Tree qualities good. Surpassed by standard sorts.
744										Supplanted by better sorts.
745										Not equal to Red Astrachan. Not recommended.
746										Has some points of merit for commercial planting.
747										Worthless.
748										Southern. Surpassed by others.
749										Value unknown. Probably obsolete.
750										Very hardy. Promising for rigorous climates.
751										Handsome but not valuable.
752										Not recommended.
753										Both tree characters and fruit poor in New York.
754	*	*		*	*	*	*	*	*	Of value for home and local market.
755										Of little value.
756										
757										Worthless.
758										Dropped from cultivation.
759										Worth planting in the home orchard.
760										Of Alexander type. Hardly worth planting.
761										Undesirable.
762	*	*		*	*	*	*	*	*	Poor cropper. Valuable in some districts. Bruises easily.
763										Much inferior to standard sorts.
764										Of no value except as a very late keeper.
765	**	**	**	**	**	*	*	*	*	One of the best extra early sorts for home and market.
766										Practically worthless.
767										

ABBREVIATIONS.— *Size.*— l, large; m, medium; s, small; v, very. *Form.*—a, angular; c, conical; l, light; r, red; ru, russet; s, striped; w, white; y, yellow. *Flavor.*— a, acid; b, brisk; m, mild; s, sweet; *Starring.*— *, recommended; **, well recommended; +, worthy of trial.

No.	VARIETY.	Origin.	Bearing age.	Form.	Size.	Color of skin.	Color of flesh.	Flavor.	Quality.	Use.	Season.
768	York	Mass.		r c	m	y b	w	sa	g—vg	k	Oct., Nov.
769	York Imperial	Pa.	5 yrs.	r o	m—l	y r s	y	m sa	g—vg	d k	Jan., Mar.
770	York Stripe	Pa.		r c	l	g y r s	w	m sa	f	k	Oct., Dec.
771	Zoar	O.	9 yrs.	r o	m	g y r	y w	sa	f	k	Nov., Dec.
772	Zolotareff	Rus.		r c	l	g y r s	g w	sa	g	k	Aug., Sept.
773	Zusoff	Rus.		r o c	l	g y d r	w	sa	g	k	Oct., Nov.
	CRABAPPLES.										
774	Algerienne	Unk.		r ov	s	g y b	g w	sa	f	k	Sept., Oct.
775	Bailey	N. Y.		r c	m—l	y r	....	sa	g	k	Oct., Dec.
776	Brier	Wis.		r c	l	y r s	y	s	g	d	Sept., Oct.
777	Cherry	Unk.		o	s	y r s	y	m sa	g	k	Aug., Oct.
778	Coral	Ill.		r o	s	y b	y	m sa	g	d	Oct., Feb.
779	Currant	Unk.		o	s	y r s	y	sa	f—p	k	Oct., Nov.
780	Dartmouth	N. H.		r o	m—l	y r	y	m sa	g	k	Aug.
781	Excelsior	Minn.		r o	l	y r	w	sa	g—vg	d k	Sept.
782	Florence	Minn.		o	m	y w r	y	b sa	g	k	Aug., Sept.
783	Gibb	Wis.		r o	l	y b r	y	sa	g	k	Aug.
784	Grant	Minn.	4 yrs.	r o	s—m	g y r s	y w	sa	f	k	Sept., Oct.
785	Hohenheimer	Unk.		r o	s	y r	y	sa	g	k	Sept., Oct.
786	Hyslop	Unk.		r c	l—m	y d r	y	sa	g	k	Sept., Oct.
787	Large Red Siberian	Unk.		r	m	y r s	y	sa	g	k	Sept., Oct.
788	Large Yellow Siberian	Unk.		r	l	y b	y	b sa	g	k	Sept., Oct.
789	Marengo	Ill.		r o	l	y r	y w	sa	g	d k	Nov., Mar.
790	Martha	Minn.		o	m—l	y r	y	b sa	g—vg	d k	Sept., Nov.
791	Minnesota	Minn.		r	l	y	w	sa	g	k	Sept., Oct.
792	Montreal	Can.		r o	l	y r	y w	b sa	g	k	Sept., Oct.
793	Oblong	Unk.		ob c	m	y w r s	....	sa	g	k	Sept.
794	Orange	Am.		r o	m	y	y w	m sa	g	k	Sept., Nov
795	Paul Imperial	Eng.		o	s—m	y r	y	b sa	g	k	Sept., Oct.
796	Picta Striata	Unk.		o	m—l	g y r s	y	sa	g	k	Oct., Dec.
797	Quaker	Unk.		r o	m—l	y b	w y	sa	f	k	Oct.
798	Queen Choice	Unk.		r c	m	y r	y	sa	g	k	Oct.
799	September	Minn.		r ob c	m—l	y r s	y	sa	g—vg	d k	Sept.
800	Soulard	Mo.		o	vl	y r	w	a	p	k	Oct., Dec.
801	Transcendent	Am.		r ob c	m—l	y b	y	sa	vg	k	Aug., Sept.
802	Van Wyck	N. Y.		r c	l	w b	w	s	g—vg	d k	Aug., Sept.
803	Whitney	Ill.		r c	l	y r s	y	m sa	g—vg	d k	Aug., Sept.
804	Yellow Siberian	Eu.		r o	m—s	y	y	sa	g	k	Sept.

i, irregular; o, oblate; ob, oblong; ov, ovate; r, roundish. *Color.*— b, blush; c, carmine; d, dark; g, green; sa, subacid. *Quality.*— b, best; g, good; f, fair; p, poor; v, very. *Use.*— d, dessert; k, kitchen.

No.	Long Island.	Hudson Valley.	St. Lawrence and Champlain Vl'ys.	Mohawk Valley.	Eastern Plateau.	Central Lakes.	Ontario Shore.	Erie Shore.	Western Plateau.	REMARKS.
768										Worthless.
769										Reports adverse to its culture in New York.
770										A worthless variety.
771										Of no value.
772										Inferior to Oldenburg.
773										Apparently surpassed by other varieties of its season.
774										Surpassed by other varieties.
775										Passed from cultivation.
776										Worthless.
777										An old variety, now little grown.
778										Worthless.
779										Very hardy but of no commercial value.
780										Lacks vigor. Excelled by other crabs.
781	*	*	*	*	*	*	*	*	*	One of the most desirable of its season.
782										Not desirable for commercial planting.
783	*	*	*	*	*	*	*	*	*	Recommended for home use and possibly for market.
784										Not recommended.
785										Not fully tested. Fruit runs small.
786	**	**	**	**	**	**	**	**	**	Widely and deservedly cultivated for home and market.
787										Better varieties are now preferred.
788										Superseded by better varieties.
789										A good late-keeping crab for home use.
790	**	**	**	**	**	**	**	**	**	One of the best.
791										Lacks productiveness at this Station.
792										Worthless.
793										Fails in New York.
794										Not recommended.
795										Does not find favor.
796										Unworthy.
797										Without special value.
798										Worthless.
799										Suitable for kitchen or dessert.
800										Has no value in the orchard.
801	**	**	**	**	**	**	**	**	**	Tree hardy, good grower, very productive. Very popular.
802										Worthless.
803	*	*	*	*	*	*	*	*	*	One of the most popular of the large crabs.
804										Valued for home use.

Made in United States
North Haven, CT
01 February 2024